MW00509632

TERRITORIAL ARMY:
FUTURE CHALLENGES

TERRITORIAL ARMY: FUTURE CHALLENGES

by

Lt Col Harish Katoch

(Established 1870)

United Service Institution of India
New Delhi

Vij Books India Pvt Ltd
New Delhi (India)

Published by

Vij Books India Pvt Ltd
(Publishers, Distributors & Importers)
2/19, Ansari Road
Delhi – 110 002
Phones: 91-11-43596460, 91-11-47340674
Fax: 91-11-47340674
e-mail: vijbooks@rediffmail.com

Copyright © 2013, United Service Institution of India, New Delhi

Paperback Edition 2015

All rights reserved.

No part of this book may be reproduced, stored in a retrieval system, transmitted or utilized in any form or by any means, electronic, mechanical, photocopying, recording or otherwise, without the prior permission of the copyright owner. Application for such permission should be addressed to the publisher.

The views expressed in the book are of the author and not necessarily those of the USI or publishers.

CONTENTS

FOREWORD

It is a distinct pleasure to sign the foreword to the book on 'Territorial Army' written by Lt Col Harish Katoch. It is a subject of much value, is contemporary and relevant in changing environment.

Throughout the last century, the phenomenon of reorganizing, down scaling or up scaling of combat forces has been seen emerging with recurring frequency. The Territorial Army itself has seen many reviews, prime ones being after the WW I, after the independence and after Operation Prakram. The US National Guards and the UK Territorial Army are again being refurbished after their experiences of the recent wars in Iraq and Afghanistan. The statecraft dictates that the prevailing warfare and defence concepts are reviewed from time to time so that they remain contemporary and relevant; and cater to futuristic environment. In this context, the Book is a valuable step forward.

Demand of forces generally exceeds supply and availability is consumed as quickly as it is established. In a security scenario which is defined by high risks through crystal gazing, there will always be thirst for greater punch; irrespective of the costs. The transformation of Army and creation of many value assets also dictate requirement of additional forces. How does one balance the equation between requirements, risks and cost? Territorial Army is one such instrument which can help in achieving the balance. Due to its inherent flexibility and ability to upscale and downscale and also its availability as a feeder to the main forces, it assumes a critical position. In the emerging scenario, requirement for specialized trades is assuming importance. Recently, the US and the UK have been looking towards creating 'Cyber National Guards/Territorials'. The advantage of local knowledge remains one of the key factors in favour of Territorial Army. As such, it becomes relevant to have a de novo look at the Territorial Army, a task which has been adequately performed by

Harish Katoch.

Harish has covered the subject of his study in a lucid manner, providing an excellent background and perspective. He has built his case for review through very apt discussion and logical arguments. Many of his suggestions and recommendations are compelling and worthy of evaluation by our planners and economists. The study could also become a precursor for further research on the micro aspects. Our strategic 'Think Tanks' and those involved in futuristic planning need to address the subject of Territorial Army more forcefully to further build on this great flexible Institution. They can find many answers to lingering problems in the Book.

It has also been a good intellectual exercise to engage with Harish Katoch during the course of discussions on the subject. I commend him for producing a valuable document on which not much material is available in the open domain.

- Major General HK Singh (Retired)

PREFACE

Coping with changing security scenario in today's context is a big challenge for our nation. The enemy can show up in its various manifestations threatening every conceivable aspect of the society. The Territorial Army (Citizens' Army) is an ideal tool which is flexible enough to fill the vacuum and cater for all asymmetric requirements in the current fluid security environment. Conventional threat will only be one part of enemy design in future conflicts. A determined enemy will try and convert any village, town or city into a potential frontier in future wars. It is with this purpose in mind that an effort has been made to address rudimentary security challenges that our country may face in future. Two of the many important challenges that our developing country is likely to face are:-

- Balancing the twin factors of 'National Security' and 'Maintaining adequate strength of Armed Forces'.

- Creation of large reserve force in the country by volunteer participation of leaders and common citizens by way of enrolling into Part-time Army (Territorial Army).

The objective of writing the book on Territorial Army is to identify futuristic requirements and potential challenges for this instrument of national importance as also to review its current organization to suggest better options for its optimal employment. The book is laid out in 12 chapters through which a graduated approach has been made to analyse the importance of people's participation in the defence of the country.

ACKNOWLEDGEMENT

'Territorial Army: Future Challenges' was written as a Research Paper based on my passion and regard for the subject. I am convinced that the concept of Territorial Army (TA) has a tremendous potential to bring the society closer to security mechanism and intertwine the citizens into defence of the country. It provides level field to all citizens to live their dream of donning military uniform on part-time basis in the service of the nation.

I am thankful to United Service Institution of India for having gauged the importance of the subject and accepting my research proposal. My sincere thanks to Major General (Retired) YK Gera, Consultant and Head (Research) and Major General (Retired) PJS Sandhu, Deputy Director and Editor for having faith in me and keeping me motivated throughout my stay at USI. They have shaped my work through their suggestions and timely advice.

The random expressions in the book contain aspirations, hope and contributions of all Territorials – serving and retired. In the absence of adequate documented material available on the subject in open domain, the solace always came from the TA fraternity in form of formal/informal contributions. I am really thankful to all those who despite their busy schedules gave me timely inputs to attempt this nascent subject. I am indebted to Brigadier (Retired) KP Singh Deo – a Terrier himself, for having spared his valuable time for chairing one of my presentations at USI and sharing his thoughts on future of TA. I sincerely thank him for encouraging and re-igniting the passion in me to write on the subject.

I take this opportunity to remember and thank my ADGs with whom I had the privilege of serving in TA Directorate. They are, Major General (Retired) P Rajagopal, AVSM, VSM, Major General (Retired) VK Datta, AVSM, SM**, VSM** and Major General (Retired) Kr VS Lalotra, AVSM, YSM, SM. They are the ones who taught to appreciate the potential of TA and enriched me with new ideas about this concept. My thanks also go towards my DDGs, Brigadier Jasjit

Singh, Brigadier later Major General (Retired) VSS Goudar, AVSM, VSM and Brigadier later Major General (Retired) HK Singh (my Project Guide) for having guided me through the learning process of TA. Here, I would specifically like to thank one of my colleagues and a dear friend in TA Directorate, Lieutenant Colonel VV Vaidya for univocally supporting me in pursuing some important proposals for TA and taking them to their logical conclusion. I am fortunate for having got full support and valuable advice for my project from Major General (Retired) Gurdeep Singh, AVSM, SM, ex ADG TA and Major General AK Siwach, YSM, VSM, the present ADG TA; I am grateful for their intellectual and moral contributions.

My gratitude and thanks to Lieutenant General (Retired) HS Lidder, PVSM, UYSM, YSM, VSM, Lieutenant General (Retired) PC Katoch, PVSM, UYSM, AVSM, SC, Major General (Retired) Dhruv Katoch, SM, VSM, Director CLAWS for having given their words of wisdom on the subject which reflect in the book. I also thank Squadron Leader (Retired) RTS Chinna, Secretary and Editor CAFHR, USI for teaching me nuances of research and assisting me in selection of material for my subject study. I was also benefitted from my fellow researchers at USI who willingly parted with the knowledge pertaining to their subject fields; which was applicable for my project. I am very thankful to all of them.

I, very sincerely thank Lieutenant General (Retired) PK Singh, PVSM, AVSM, Director, USI for involving himself in my project study and giving very valuable recommendations from time to time. He, in fact, told me to think out of the box to address various facets of my study.

Lastly, I profusely thank my Project Guide, Major General (Retired) HK Singh for guiding me from inception stage of the project study till its last day. His in-depth knowledge on TA coupled with his unbiased and critical comments have helped in shaping my study and bringing spontaneity and interest in the work.

It will not be fair if I reserve my appreciation for the sustained support from my wife, Anuradha and daughter, Chitralekha who always encouraged me and kept me focused on my project.

- Harish Katoch

ABBREVIATIONS

AD	-	Air Defence
ASEC	-	Army Standing Establishment Committee
ARNG	-	Army National arfare StudieGuard
CLAWS	-	Centre for Land and Air Warfare Studies
DSC	-	Defence Security Corps
EME	-	Electronic and Mechanical Engineers
ETF	-	Ecological Task Force
GREF	-	General Reserve Engineer Force
H&H	-	Home and Hearth
IB	-	International Border
LOC/LC	-	Line of Control
NCC	-	National Cadet Corps
NDMA	-	National Disaster Management Authority
NOC	-	No Objection Certificate
PLA	-	People's Liberation Army
RA	-	Regular Army
RAPIDS	-	Reorganised Army Plains Infantry Division
SSB	-	Services Selection Board
TA	-	Territorial Army
TNF	-	Territorial Naval Force
UTC	-	University Training Corps
VAs/VPs	-	Vulnerable Areas/ Vulnerable Points

CHAPTER I

INTRODUCTION AND HISTORICAL PERSPECTIVE

"It is the soldier, not the reporter who has given us the freedom of the press. It is the soldier, not the poet, who has given us the freedom of speech. It is the soldier, not the campus organizer, who gives us freedom to demonstrate. It is the soldier who salutes the flag, who serves beneath the flag, and whose coffin is draped by the flag, who allows the protester to burn the flag."

- Father Dennis Edward O'Brien, USMC

Background

Human species is a unique creation of nature that has been bestowed with high intelligence quotient, power of discrimination and social awareness. This combination motivates humans to live in groups and defend themselves against external hostile factors. One of the basic characteristics of human beings is to love one another and live in peace. However, contradicting this philosophy and overriding his basic nature, the man starts planning for expansion of his food needs and living boundaries in the name of survival; leading to uncalled for rivalry with others. Graduating from stone- age to present age, the mankind has seen many a tragedy filled with horror and hatred between communities and civilizations. The wars, at times have been fought on trivial territorial issues setting aside all dignity and respect for human life. The fear of annihilation and obliteration compelled right thinking communities to get together and stay in peace as bigger nations. This social integration has been a great step in the history of mankind. But despite all this good, the insecurity still persists among the nations and wars are still fought. Each country maintains its separate army to safeguard its boundaries and as a result, a good amount of money is spent on sustenance of armies all over the world.

The evolution of mankind has been an historical phenomenon. The history of evolution is a reservoir of experiences that allows new generations to glance through in the past and appreciate insatiable aspirations of human civilizations. It will be realized that the bottom line has all along been, empowerment through expansion. For this singular passion, wars have been fought since time immemorial. As the time passed, social developments took place and man learnt to stay in planned civil societies. With this development, he improvised on the defence sets up of his community and society. Organised armies came into being with the main aim of safeguarding own territories against external aggressions. Though the primary obligation of fighting battles and wars all along remained with enrolled soldiers of state armies yet history is full of incidents where to safeguard the honour of the motherland, the common citizens of societies picked up arms against a superior enemy force and fought alongside their armies to defeat the enemy. References of such volunteer support by local population during wars exist in Ramayana and Mahabharata as also during Aacharya Chanakya's time when he garnered the support of local citizens against Alexander. Local citizen-soldiers have always played a vital role in the defence of the motherland especially in Indian context. The volunteer duty rendered by a common citizen fighting as a soldier for the honour of the country remains his prized possession.

Nations all over the world have their national security mechanisms in place against unforeseen external and internal threats. Some countries have manpower intensive security system based on large standing armies whereas some others have manageable standing armies ably assisted by large reserves. The type of security requirements for each country may be unique based on different geographical, social and political conditions. A country with long borders with its difficult neighbours may have different compulsions vis-a-vis a country which is at peace with its neighbourhood. Other than these compulsions, some countries that have expansion plans and have their interests to be safeguarded at far off regions will have larger armies by going in for compulsory enrolment for their citizens.

A large number of countries including developed countries have realized the non-viability of maintaining large standing armies at all times. They appreciate that it is much easier to manage comparatively smaller army and in turn have large reserves by way of having volunteer army whose men come for few months in a year for routine training, as per their convenience. This option provides to the common citizens a platform to be part of the national defence. In a way, the security of the country goes down to each and every family of the country.

The defence of a nation is a dynamic process and is increasingly becoming collective responsibility of all citizens. The future wars are going to be multi-dimensional and will require multi-faceted forces and technological parameters to counter them. For this reason, countries with foresight and well chalked out developmental plans, keep maximum of their citizens trained for military duties and hold them as a large reserve; ready for wartime requirements and unforeseen national emergencies. Mobilising such trained people within required areas is much faster and easier. This practice has existed in our country since the times of Maharajas. The obligation of providing able bodied fighters for war time requirement used to be clearly spelt out and distributed amongst Senapatis and Jagirdars who further distributed this down to village heads. The complete population in this way was involved with the security of the state. Besides, these warriors were present in their villages when not called upon by the king, for ensuring peace and harmony in the society as also providing intelligence to the royal administration.

In modern times also, to deal with any external threat to national integrity and/or any national emergency in terms of natural disasters or unusual internal problems, no sovereign country will have plans to completely depend on its regular armed forces. Direct or indirect support from the civil population is essential to complement the overall effort. A local component from the civil society, as an additional force will always be of great help. In fact, the regular army can never be at all the places at all the times. Therefore, it is extremely important to have regional defence sets up in place as volunteer part-time force.

We, in India have such a force existing since pre independence in the form of the Territorial Army (TA).

India, Down the Ages

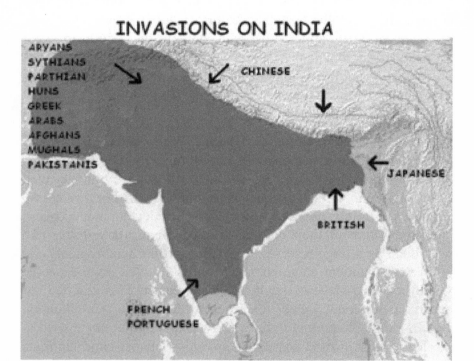

Map 1

Indian soil has seen numerous rulers and dynasties in the past. Many invader armies at different times were able to penetrate its sovereignty and take possession of the vast resources it offered. This land has been subjected to organized loot by all occupational forces. But, whenever the people of India stood together and fought united, the country did well and finally for this reason, got much awaited independence in 1947 from British rule.

Evolution of TA in India

Volunteer participation by civil population in battles and wars is an historical fact in India, however, the organized participation of civilians in India with the aim of supplementing the regular army is comparatively recent and dates back to 1857. Before 1857, the British

Empire in India seemed to have complete control over Indians, its states and feudal kings. In the name of actual power sharing, there was really no native representation in the administration at higher levels and Indians were generally placed at subordinate levels. When the uprising of 1857 was underway, the British administration was, somehow, successful in keeping it contained to affected regions. The movement could not become an integrated, well-coordinated and simultaneous affair. Local leaders could not foresee and gauge the enthusiasm of the people and failed to bring infuriated masses under one banner to give direction to their patriotic outbursts. The countrymen had to pay heavily for this omission; both, during and post uprising in terms of physical losses and more humiliating life respectively. The seed of freedom, however, had been sown!

1857 revolution was a big jolt to British administration and its intelligence agencies. Immediately after the failed uprising, serious efforts were made to prevent such reoccurrences in future. It was felt necessary by the British administration to create a mechanism that could directly sense the aspirations of the people and any unrest developing in their minds. To this end, an organized volunteer force comprising of Europeans and Anglo-Indians, came into being in 1857. The primary object of the Force was to assist government and ensure the safety and well-being of European British subjects in the event of general disorder.[1] The force included infantry regiments, mounted regiments and artillery. Later, the domain was expanded and big railway companies operating in India raised their battalion from railway personnel in 1869. All units and people forming part of the force were called as, 'Volunteers'. These battalions were recruited and organized on the same lines as regular units of the British army. They were trained primarily for local territorial security and for feeling the pulse of natives. To have an army imprint on these units, an officer each from regular units was provided as adjutant to function as a nucleus. The enrolment, training and efficiency matrix for units was not centrally defined and therefore, varied considerably in each unit. The concept was termed successful as enough volunteers opted for

---

[1] Reorganisation of the Army and Air Force in India; Report of a Committee set up by H E Gen Sir Claude J E Auchinleck, GCB, GCIE, CSI, DSO, OBE, ADC, Commander in Chief; Vol I, Para 82, page No 28.

enrolment in these units. However, the handicaps of employment of these units only to limited areas with limited obligations were felt during deployment of army in WW I. Volunteers till now had not been used as collective units outside assigned territories. The regulations thus needed amendments. That was the time when idea of compulsory service was mooted by public bodies and redefining of role and obligation of this force was considered necessary by the government.[2] This led to passage of, 'Indian Defence Force Act' in 1917. This Act introduced a compulsory service for European British subjects in India as a war measure for Imperial emergency. The Act remained in force till 1920, with various amendments concerning the age up to which men should serve, and the territorial limitations of service. This Act was replaced by another Act in 1920 called as, 'Auxiliary Force Act' which enabled a constitution of an Auxiliary Force in India. Under this Act, compulsory service was abolished and volunteers were encouraged to join. Under this Act also, the membership in Auxiliary Force was accessible to only European British subjects. This was an improved version where service liabilities and training were clearly defined. [3]

Almost concurrently, in 1920, the history took a positive turn for India and brought a big opportunity. Based on Montagu-Chelmsford reforms concerning national security, Indian Territorial Force Act was passed. The reforms were based on the logic that self-government could not be a complete reality without the capacity for self defence. The force to be raised under this Act was intended to cater, amongst other things, for the military aspirations of those classes of population to whom military service had not hitherto been a hereditary profession.[4] It was intended, at the same time, to be a second line to, and a source of reinforcement for, the regular Indian Army. Membership of the force for this latter reason carried with it a liability for something more than purely local service or home defence. It intended, in some circumstances, service overseas.[5] This

---

[2] The Army in India And Its Evolution, Calcutta : Superintendent Government Printing, India – 1924.

[3] Ibid

[4] Ibid

[5] Ibid

Act brought the complete society closer to the defence establishment. This was a step towards Indianisation of military services. The idea was to embody volunteers for short periods every year during peace and enable them to undertake short and intense training to be able to function alongside army during war. This Force started with two main components; namely University Training Corps (UTC) and Provincial Battalions. Whereas the members of UTC were drawn from staff and students of universities whose liability finished with their exit from the institution, the members of provincial battalions were from all walks of society and had full service liability. The members of UTC were trained by British instructors and were the potential pool of disciplined and educated candidates for provincial battalions. The training staff for members of provincial battalions, on the other hand, consisted of regular Indian officers and Other Rank loaned by their units for the purpose. Men were enrolled in provincial battalions for a period of six years, this period was even reduced to four years in certain cases. On the completion of first engagement period, they could again enroll voluntarily, for further specified periods. During his first year, every man did twenty-eight days preliminary training, and in every subsequent year he received periodical training for the same duration. During embodiment for training, the Indian ranks were treated as regards pay, discipline etc. at par with the ranks of regular Indian Army. Later, on the recommendations of The Shea Committee which was constituted in 1924 to suggest steps to improve and enlarge the Indian Territorial Force, the Provincial component was bisected and two types of units namely; Urban units and Provincial units came into being.

CHAPTER II

FORMALISATION AND GROWTH OF TERRITORIAL ARMY POST INDEPENDENCE

"It does not interfere with peaceful vocations and at the same time, trains a person for national service, thus not only preparing them for emergency but making them better citizens."

- Pandit Jawahar Lal Nehru

Territorial Army of India

After independence of India in 1947, the structure of the army did not change much and it was decided to continue with the prevailing system which contained within it the following components:-

(a) Regular Army (RA)

(b) Army Reserve

(c) Territorial Army (TA)

This was the time when there was an echo in the society for providing military training to the civil population. This was based on the desire among the people to be part of nation's defence set-up coupled with their zeal to have disciplined, dignified, adventurous and an orderly life style. Debates were held on having large standing army on permanent basis vis-à-vis small functional army assisted by reserves in form of adequate and larger TA component which could be mobilized easily; as on required basis. The latter option was felt to be right choice for the newly born country.

1947-1964

After independence, it was appreciated that Indian Territorial Force Act of 1920 was not adequate for Indian Army and needed clear objectives as per country's needs. This resulted in bringing into being, 'Territorial Army Act of 1948'. Consequently, the UTC was converted into National Cadet Corps for students and staff of colleges and universities all over India and Territorial Army became a separate entity. On what should be the structure of Indian Army, the Territorial Act of 1948 had envisaged a TA of approximately 1.37 lakh as compared to the then regular army of three lakh[1] to safeguard the frontiers of the nation.

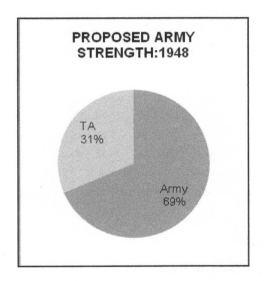

PROPOSED ARMY STRENGTH:1948

After 1949, the making up of deficiencies in regular army and the expansion of TA commenced. In 1952, Reserve and Auxiliary Air Force Act was enacted. Seven Auxiliary Air Force Squadrons were raised at different cities. The volunteers who were part of these squadrons were called Part Time Flyers. This Act brought in a lot of enthusiasm in the society. After 1962 debacle however, these squadrons were absorbed into regular Air Force. In 1955, an unwritten

---

[1] Citizens' Army – a Coffee Table book on TA by Additional Directorate General TA, page 9 and 22.

review of TA was done and steadily growing TA got a setback in terms of equipment and manpower. There were certain reductions in the scale of equipment and redundant personnel were disposed off. Armour and Army Supply Corps units were disbanded. During the same year, the TA was expanded by raising National Volunteer Force (later designated as Lok Sahayak Sena) with a view to imparting rudimentary military training to volunteers in the society. Under this scheme, over seven lakh volunteers were trained.[2] While addressing the first National Volunteer Camp at Delhi on 1 May 1955, the then Defence Minister, Mr Kailash Nath Katju had said, "What people will, I imagine value the most, is the new opportunity made available to them for leading a disciplined life for a month and undergoing training in a camp under supervision. I am sure that this Volunteer Force will capture the imagination of the people and the demand for further expansion will be great everywhere throughout India."

It must be recalled here that the defence policy of the country after independence was based on total idealism and was far away from ground realities. The casual and unrealistic assessment of army strength coupled with its poor equipment profile was totally exposed during 1962 Chinese aggression. The defeat, in a way could be termed as a much required catalyst for initiating the modernization and focused military training of the Indian Army.

1965-1980

By 1962, the TA had added more number of units and they took active part in operations acquitting themselves very well. Later, TA further expanded alongside regular army and added many types of units, largely infantry units. During 1965 war, TA units took active part in relieving army units from their static duties including prestigious Rashtrapati Bhawan special guard.

---

[2] Citizens' Army – a Coffee Table book on TA by Additional Directorate General TA, page 24

1965 – TA Unit Relieving Rashtrapati Bhawan Guard

TA Air Defence Detachment

TA Air Defence detachments actively participated in operations and did extremely well.[3] Seeing growing importance of TA within national security matrix, TA Group Headquarters were raised at various HQ Commands in 1968 for coordinated functioning of TA resources under them. TA was at its peak strength during 1971 war

---

[3]   Citizens' Army – a Coffee Table book on TA by Additional Directorate General TA, page 26

with Pakistan when it participated in both Eastern and Western fronts. After 1971 operations when ceasefire was declared, bulk of TA units were committed on the ceasefire line, and because of regular requirement of troops there, most of them were absorbed in regular army. Subsequently, some units were disbanded also as their operational requirement was no longer felt necessary.

1981-2000

An all-important era of 'Greening India' started in 1982 with the raising of first Ecological TA Battalion (based on ex-servicemen) at Dehradun. The success of the mission has been appreciated by one and all. In fact, this battalion has become a role model not only for Indian states but for countries across the world. The success of the concept led to raising of more such Task Forces and today, TA has eight ecological battalions operating in different states. These Task Forces were able to plant and nurture approximately five crore saplings in over 51,000 hectares of land (status as of 31 Dec 2012). On the performance of Ecological Battalions, Gen BC Joshi, the ex-Chief of Army Staff had following to say, "The Territorial Army is playing a commendable role alongside the Regular Army and has acquitted itself with credit in troubled areas of our country. I am particularly pleased to see its contribution in the field of ecology in which its performance has been outstanding." TA units during these two decades also participated in overseas peace keeping duties alongside regular army during Operation Pawan in Sri Lanka and later in active operations during Operation Vijay in 1999.

2001-2012

The new millennium started with TA being deployed for Operation Prakram in 2001. Here, TA stood shoulder to shoulder with regular army and was able to fully relieve regular troops for their operational tasks well within given time. On the basis of lessons learnt from these operations, 'Home & Hearth' TA units were conceived and raised 2004 onwards. These units are based on 'sons of soil' concept and draw their troops from the local areas that they intend to defend. So far they have yielded desired results but need revaluation and re-tasking now.

As mentioned earlier, the Indian Territorial Force initially consisted of two main categories, Provincial Battalions and University Training Corps Battalions. It is through University Training Corps Battalions that the youth studying in colleges and universities was intended to be motivated to join defence services of the country. The liability of the members, however, was restricted and they were discharged of their liability on ceasing to belong to the university. The intention was not to enforce the liability on the members to render actual military service. The intention however was, in addition to inculcating disciplined life and character building, to prepare them to be a source of supply of officers and men for the Provincial Battalions where the members had full liability for military service. This worked very well till 1942. In this year, University Training Corps was rechristened as University Officers Training Corps. Later, in 1946-47, the work was done to create a separate establishment capable of training and motivating the youth of the country and this is how NCC came into being in 1948. Almost concurrently, the Indian Territorial Act was passed in the same year and due to this, TA and NCC became two separate entities under MoD.

It can be concluded from the above churning that common citizen of the society, whether student or professional, was always kept in the forefront as regards defence of the country. Considering the thrust of both TA and NCC, focused on national defence, it will not at all be a bad idea to again amalgamate both and bring under one umbrella. Since aim of both is common and both are volunteer in nature, their potential to complement each other can be constructively exploited by bringing them together. This will lead to better synergy which in turn will enhance absorption of more school/ college leaving cadets into regular army or TA as they would be functioning within single system. Even if total amalgamation is not feasible, there is still a need to have inter-operability between the two.

TA – a Citizens' Force

In India, volunteer participation of common citizens during wars against external aggressions, was a way of life. The country has been mostly ruled by kings and emperors where the emphasis was given on security of people. Therefore, the recruitment, training and war worthiness of the army used to be given highest priority. The cabinet of the king was amply represented by army generals in addition to other ministers while taking decisions of national importance. The king himself had to be a qualified soldier adept in warfare. This was due to the fact that firstly, unless he knew the nuances of warfare himself, he would not be in a position to take correct decisions pertaining to the security; and secondly, by being a soldier, he would identify with his army in a better way and command his authority as an able warrior-leader. The army was placed at an elevated social pedestal so that the citizens of the state would aspire to be a part of it. It was known to them that development of the state was only possible when it had a strong army. For developing able bodied soldiers having agility and presence of mind; sports, based on sword fighting, riding, archery and wrestling were propagated in the society to enable citizens to remain fit to be able to pick up arms if situation so desired.

After independence when India evolved as a Union, it was felt necessary to have societal participation in defence of the country. In order to keep the complete society in touch with its armed forces, the idea of strengthening the TA concept was propagated in India. The TA is a part-time volunteer army where people employed in other professions come to give their services in uniform. Because of its deep down reach in the society and its connect with citizens, this army is also popularly called, Citizens' Army. The enrolment in this army is zonal based and any fit candidate from any section of society between 18- 42 years of age is eligible to be enrolled.

Is Introduction of Technology in Army Paving Way for TA-isation?

With the introduction of simulators and computers in Army at Unit/ Subunit levels, Training Centres, Records and Depots managing big inventories, it was presumed that with passage of time, things would stabilize and some staff would become surplus. However, this is not visible. Taking an example of computer, the facility could not be used to the advantage and machines were not exploited by the users to reduce paper work. In fact, the work got doubled as for every document created and forwarded, a hard copy is posted to all concerned and an office copy is filed. The organization has failed in training its staff to adapt to the new medium effectively. Coming to EME, whereas the repair and maintenance of IT and related technical equipment should be outsourced to the supplying agencies, army itself is busy creating manpower intensive infrastructure for accounting and maintenance of variety of equipment purchased from different agencies. The automation of signal exchanges and other advancements in signal equipment has not brought down strength in Signal units. There are numerous such places where man power could be reduced and sidestepped to other places requiring more manpower. As an organization, we have to ponder over these issues and identify dormant staff to channelize it in right direction. The mindset of staff officers wanting to have a separate helper, runner, clerk and staff to themselves, has to somehow, change.

Why has TA Concept Not Taken off Successfully in India?

We, the people of India are generally impulsive in nature; this reflects in our personality and conduct as well. Our national decisions are mostly taken in hurry and due to this reason, lack far-sightedness. We were a worried class when the British created Auxiliary Force for themselves in 1857 which continued till 1920. We badly wanted this Force to have our countrymen also, as part of it. Once it was created in 1920 for us, we were relieved and performed very well till independence. Because of the genuine keenness of countrymen towards the concept, Indian Territorial Act was passed in 1948 and it was presumed that volunteers from various departments would come in hoards. However, as the generations followed and spirit of freedom movement started waning in the hearts and minds of youth, the defence of the country started taking back seat and more and more people started concentrating on alluring commercial activities. Slowly, the instrument of TA given as a unique gift to the society started losing its charm; and today, the outfit has over 40 percent shortage of officers. The people of the society alone cannot be blamed for this as there have been many volunteer employees in almost all departments who still wish to join TA. But due to lack of timely amendments in existing TA Rules and Regulations connected to enrolment and employment of personnel, the number of applicants has come down. The responsibility for this omission lies both with the Government and the Army. In addition, the bureaucracy has also not played its part responsibly. Advertently or inadvertently, there has been a collective failure in correctly setting the priorities and reading the aspirations of the people. Because of such indifference, this excellent organization had to traverse a very difficult path in past years. There are numerous reasons for this failure but some of the glaring ones that need immediate attention are listed below:-

(a)   Apathy on Government's Part

(i)   The TA Act passed in 1948 was reviewed thrice for its effectiveness and to further draw out a road map for expansion of TA and its future employment, however, as a follow up, no concrete results were seen on ground.

(ii)   The recruitment was totally left on individual's choice and no attention was paid towards employers who had to spare their employees and issue them the mandatory NOC on annual basis. This has resulted into non-cooperation from employers' side. An effort to work out some solution by having mutual discussions with private players across the board, has never been made.

(iii)   Central and state government employees who are directly dealing with MoD and should be at the center stage for enrolment in TA as part-timers, have no liability to serve the organization for any specified minimum period during their civil careers. Some provision should be made for these employees to render their services in TA for 4-5 years before acquiring a specified age. An additional increment in current salary or pension and any other promotional benefit to these employees in their parent departments can go a long way in attracting them towards Citizens' Army.

(b)   Failure on Army Side

(i)   The expansion of TA as a tool for augmenting Army's efforts in war and emergencies has not been perceived in right perspective. Any proposal on expansion is always taken as a threat towards downsizing of army. This being the conceptual indifference, the expansion of TA will never be possible. It is high time TA is expanded horizontally to relieve regular army of mundane duties that are coming in its way as a routine and distracting it from its primary task and training.

(ii)   There is no road map in the army as regards utilization of old equipment shed by heavy equipment intensive units on their getting new equipment. The old equipment can be optimally utilized by raising TA units of such regiments. The creation of reserve force based on Armour, Artillary, AD and Engineer regiments making use of this equipment can be an excellent addition.

(iii)   At present, it is being made to believe that army cannot be expanded beyond its present strength and 'Save and Raise' is the basis spelt out for new raisings. If that is the binding, it will be a good idea to examine if more units with troops coming under Composite Tables II of manpower can be raised.

(c) Non-Participation by Political Leaders and Bureaucrats. In US, many members from political parties and civil services are enrolled in their National Guard - equivalent of our TA. It is a matter of pride for US that out of their 44 Presidents, 20 had been officers in their National Guard/ Militia. The difficulties faced by soldiers in field conditions were experienced by many of them which made their decision about their forces that much easier. The same is the case in UK. The Royal family still takes pride in actively associating itself with the Armed Forces of their country. Prince William and Harry are the latest examples. It is ironic that political class and bureaucracy in our country do not feel any obligation to serve the defence forces. Very few politicians who alongside their political careers served TA as officers can be counted on fingers. These are:-

(i)   Brig (Retd) K P Singh Deo, AVSM

(ii)   Late Brig P S Rathore, VSM

(iii)   Late Capt Rao Birender Singh

(iv)   Capt (Retd) Sanjay Singh

(v)   Brig (Retd) S S Sawant

(vi)   Maj D Y Sema

(vii)   Maj Manvendra Singh

(viii)   Lt Sachin Pilot

A spirited presentation was made to young MPs in 2009 in South Block auditorium in the presence of Dr Pallam Raju, Raksha Rajaya Mantri and the Chief of Army Staff to give them an overview on importance of societal participation in the defence set up of the country and motivate them to join TA. A lot of queries came thereafter from many quarters but the result so far has been only one MP in Shri Sachin Pilot. In the absence of initiative to join TA from political leaders and bureaucrats, some renowned personalities from sports and cine world were granted President's Honorary Commission in recent years in order to popularize the concept of Citizens' Army. More proactive approach in this regard by reaching out to young people in schools and colleges will be helpful.

As regards bureaucrats joining TA, the boundaries of seniority and superiority between defence and civil services are so water tight that no member from this fraternity will join this Force at his own. The already explained statuary binding for compulsory military service of limited periods for Central Government employees in TA is the answer which can transform the Force and will accrue intangible results for the nation in the long run.

CHAPTER III

RELEVANCE OF TERRITORIAL ARMY IN PRESENT SECURITY SCENARIO

"Every Territorial is twice a citizen, once when he does his ordinary job and the second time when he dons his uniform and plays his part in defence."

- Field Marshal Viscount Slim

Concept of TA

The conceptual framework for the TA is based on the fundamental idea that it should exist for war time employment and should be maintainable at the lowest cost during peace time. The concept encompasses the employment of disciplined, trained, dedicated and a low cost force of country's citizens drawn from all walks of life to support, supplement and augment the resources of regular army. Being trained for war, this force is capable of performing tasks which the regular army units are called upon to perform during peace and national emergencies. This force also provides surge capability to the army in times of increased requirement with respect to ready availability of reserve force or/and to build up more regular units on existing TA units.

The concept provides unique platform to the gainfully employed citizens in becoming competent soldiers as a result of military training imparted to them. The force thus enables reduction in manpower costs during peace time, as its personnel are required to come for their annual training for only two months every year as compared to regular army units, which remain full strength throughout the year.

What is TA-isation?

The word 'TA-isation' is derived from acronym of Territorial Army – TA. As the word 'TA' indicates part-time nature of its job, the 'TA-isation' indicates presence of part-time element in an organization. The TA-isation within an organization is the flexibility that it has to utilize its minimum resources to achieve maximum results yet be in a position to retain the ability to muster up its reserve strength with ease, when situation so demands. Today, on seeing around, the success manatra in all production related organisations and rapidly expanding corporate world is their forethought and judicious use of human resource. In armed forces, leaving aside TA units which as per their obligation have to follow part-time schedules of training and employment, many areas in regular units can also be identified where man power could be enrolled on part-time basis for peace time duties and kept ready to be used for war time emergencies, as is done in TA battalions.

Is TA Really Required in the Country?

It may be a debatable point as to why the idea of TA-isation is being discussed and propagated at the first place in our country where there is no dearth of eligible manpower for recruitment in the army and people are readily available at any instant. It is a fact that army recruitment in any corner of the country attracts local youth in thousands even for very few vacancies. But then, why depend on TA? If employment of TA units of past few years is any indication, almost 80 percent strength is embodied at any point and time. In light of such engagement, is it not right to convert TA units into regular units to meet operational requirements? With present arrangement, there is duplicity by maintaining two distinct establishments with no cost saving to the exchequer. If that be the case, is it not high time that the country hands over all security related issues to regular armed forces and they solely should be made accountable and answerable? This will ideally lead to compact Armed Forces establishment which has a well laid down training schedule and single command and control structure in place. This will also, in a way, steer clear the armed forces of societal closeness which, as some claim, has detrimental effects on its functioning.

The above given logic is very correct academically but unfortunately, the defence of the country is not a deal that is made with a singular organization; rather it is all inclusive. Like, for disaster and earthquake management, the country keeps plans ready in advance and makes local population undergo rehearsals and mock drills; in the same way, more and more people need to be kept trained for the defence of the country. The armed forces, responsible for the defence of the country, alone may not be in a position to meet prolonged war requirements; they need assistance from fellow citizens in many aspects. Though, the defence of the country seems to be a non-productive expenditure at first sight, but, its presence and preparedness itself is a big deterrent against divisive forces within and without.

The main reason of our youth joining armed forces is employment necessities rather than choice. Fortunately, the youth is still motivated towards armed forces as educational advancements and absorption in other sectors has not reached deep into the society. The day is not far off when the country will grow industrially and academically and priorities of youth will shift for easier and so called white collared jobs. It is a fact that we as a nation are lucky to have readily available eligible youth for recruitment into our armed forces. But it does not mean that we can enroll everyone and have huge standing army. The nation has got to have a balance in all sectors. Also, raising a larger army may be easier but its sustenance is the problem. Therefore, it may be better to have a well-equipped smaller army than to have ill-equipped larger army, in national interest.

Present Security Scenario

At the end of twentieth century, it was believed that the new century would bring in the much awaited peace and order in the world and nations would shun the path of violence that leads to conflicts and wars. But, that was not to be. The first decade of the new century seemed to be an extension of previous one as many nations kept engaged in conflicts and use of force was rampant. There have been positive changes also and citizens of many smaller countries stood up to their basic right of self-governance and have uprooted old anarchical and dictatorial regimes. There is a silver lining and it is appreciated that in times to come, the world would be a better place to live in; where misunderstandings amongst nation states would be resolved in more civilized manner across the table and not in the battle fields. Notwithstanding, the countries would still have to maintain armies for the security of their frontiers. This is because, no country can ever achieve economic independence, cultural prosperity and technological up gradation unless its frontiers are secure and there is no possibility of external interference into its progress. For this reason, countries attach greater importance towards the aspect of security.

The strength of armed forces to be maintained by any country will be directly proportional to its size, population and the extent of its land and sea borders. As maintaining an army is a costly proposition, there has to be a fine balance between the national spending on defence forces and other development activities in the country. It will be detrimental to have large armed forces, which are difficult to sustain, at the cost of progress of the country.

India has about 15,000 km of land border and 7,500km of sea coast to defend. After India got independence in 1947, our leaders promptly focused on social restructuring and industrial development of the country; missing out on a very important aspect of national security and military up gradation. It was decided that the country would have only three lakh regular army and 1.37 lakh (31%) soldiers as part-timers (TA).[1] This miscalculation of regular army weighed very heavily on the nation when China enforced war in 1962. This humiliation woke up India towards national security and finally led to expansion and modernization of armed forces in the country. Thereafter, in later conflicts, Indian forces acquitted very well, both in 1965 and 1971 against Pakistan.

Presently, India has a total of 13.25 lakh active soldiers in armed forces. Out of this, 11.2 lakh is the share of army.[2] Though, maintaining such a huge force at all times is extremely challenging yet considering upward moving Indian economic growth coupled with its enhanced role in world affairs and increased aspirations in the region,

---

[1] The Citizens' Army – a coffee table book on TA by Additional Directorate General Territorial Army.

[2] Indian Armed Forces – Wikipedia, the free Encyclopedia.

ways and means have to be found out to create adequate force, both for own national security and for peace keeping missions being an important UN member. The cap imposed by the Government on size of our armed forces must have been based on keeping conventional wars in view. However, with ever increasing threat by terrorist organisations within the country, a need has arisen to address this new dimension. This threat does not come through conventional borders alone and hence, Quick Reaction Forces have to be located closer to all sensitive areas and installations.

The proxy war initiated against India by its neighbours based on terrorist philosophy has over stretched its defence forces. So called, 'peace tenures' for army units are shrinking by the day. The only consolation that could be derived out of this melee is that Indian Army is now fully trained on counter terrorist operations. In war against terrorism, conventions on war are not complied by terrorist outfits and hence, their approach is not restricted to borders alone. They could strike at the place of their choice with impunity. This puts tremendous pressure on security forces and brings them face to face with civil population while progressing there internal security operations; causing great inconvenience to them. Because of peculiar nature of such operations, the action taken by security forces is invariably reactive and delayed. The commitment of army in North and North-Eastern parts of the country for IB/LOC security and while dealing with internal problems, compels the leadership to make available more and more troops. The present strength of over 11 lakh army, at times, seems inadequate!! New ways and means, therefore, need to be devised to restructure the security forces and make them more functional. Certain internal security duties and disaster related tasks need to be handed over for execution to the part-time army - TA. In addition, the existing role of TA of being second line force meant only for guard/escort duties in rear areas, is required to be upgraded to more important tasks where it can be used in defensive role. This will give a big reprieve to regular army from routine deployment on Road Opening duties and such like other tasks. The expansion of TA over and above the international cap, if any, will not be a problem as TA comes under Composite Table II strength and not under Composite Table I like regular army. In the interim, if situation improves and warrants down sizing of army, grades and trades in various regular Regiments/Units can be pre identified for subsequent TA-isation.

Can Army be Everywhere?

It is a myth that any frontier can be hermetically sealed by security forces. Borders will always remain porous as every inch of ground cannot be practically guarded. The inhospitable stretches of terrain along our North and North Eastern borders can best be defended by deploying units and troops much behind, where they are administratively secure and can be easily sustained. With the technological advancements and flurry of satellites at our disposal, physical deployment of troops at the borders is no more required. A particular sector can be easily monitored and dominated by lesser number of personnel, specialized in surveillance and use of precision weapon systems. No country, however rich, can think of maintaining a round the clock vigil by way of physical presence of troops at its long borders; it will neither be practical nor cost effective. The cost required for acquiring state of art surveillance equipment and precision weapon systems, on the other hand, can be offset by reducing manpower accordingly.

Army Unit during Delhi Common Wealth Games

Today, it has become a trend to call army for any emergency in the country starting from flood relief, earthquakes and internal security to organizing big events at national level. The day is not far off when the Army will be fully involved in operations against Maoists. Such gross distractions are detrimental for preparedness of army towards its primary task. It must be fully realized that army cannot be everywhere. It is not that it is incapable of executing tasks entrusted to it, but the current trend is surely a step towards weakening the agencies responsible for civil duties and making them more and more dependent on army for future. The need of the hour is to have dual task TA units raised on Home and Hearth concept. During normal times, they function on reduced strength as per TA concept and for any emergency, are immediately embodied to meet the challenges. These units need to be equipped accordingly, as per their envisaged task. The times of classical mobilization and induction of army units from far off cantonments for a particular task in remote/difficult areas are over. The requirement, today, is of handy reserve units of army that can be called upon to address the emergent requirements at the earliest.

Why is TA-isation a Viable Option?

No organization can remain on its peak efficiency throughout. The intermediary objective evaluation and subsequent course correction is mandatory to succeed. The efforts put in, need to be in consonance with the desired objectives. It is also not wise to squander away resources when output requirements need scaling down. To this end, efficient organizations commit only that much effort which brings them desired output. The Army as an organization is no exception to this rule. Here also, when there are no emergencies or war, certain identified cadres, not required on routine basis during peace times can be considered to be set aside and sent back with the premise of training them during the year for a minimum stipulated duration. This will enable them to be in touch with their trade and operational tasks. Debates at appropriate levels can be held to weigh the pros and cons of TA-ising part of the Army or for raising more TA units in future as part of army expansion plan. Also, suitable amendments can be incorporated in existing TA rules and regulations to make it more attractive and citizen-friendly.

TA – a Force in Being

TA being a part of the Army has an added advantage of having character and ethos of Army but an altogether different enrolment and employment procedure in its units. Its unique character enables it to reach out to almost all types of service classes in civil society. It will not be correct to state at this point that as mandated, only gainfully employed citizens from all walks of life join this Force driven by their passion to serve the country. Most of the volunteers who presently join have started seeing TA as a career. This has been primarily due to regular and prolonged embodiments of TA units in the past years. This trend will erode the very concept of TA and part-time aspirants will not join for fear of being embodied for longer durations and being away from their actual vocations. Anyway, if TA is seen in national context and as reinforcement for regular army during war, things would be understood in right perspective.

Unlike regular army infantry units, TA infantry units have their permanently earmarked locations assigned to them. These are based on the troop composition of the unit and its catchment area for recruitment. An effort has been made to make this Force as a pan India entity for giving representation to all segments of society to join their hands in securing the nation. Because of permanent locations of TA units, their unit headquarters generally function as mini Training Centers having requisite assets needed for training of newly recruited members. The respective state governments where these units are located, start owning them up and identify with them. This brings in a sense of pride and security amongst common citizens of the society for they know that during any emergency, TA volunteers will be available to take control of the situation.

On the conventional front also, TA units are always taken into account as a relief of regular troops; engaged in rear areas on security duties and other area domination tasks. TA units have their role, task and time frame of being effective, specified in advance for war time situations and is reflected in overall mobilization matrix.

Low Cost Option

TA units are generally organized like regular army units with some exceptions in equipment holding. Other than their personnel on permanent staff, which is a mix of regulars on loan from army units and TA cadres, all other members are part-time. They come to their units for two months in a year for refreshing their training skills and go back to their civil vocations. For the time spent in their units, they are paid out of defence accounts as per the scale applicable to regulars. The difference in initial raising cost between a TA unit and a regular unit is not much pronounced but the difference in recurring expenditure is enormous. A trained force with least liability is relevant for a developing country like ours.

For TA personnel to be eligible for pension benefits, they need to have 15 years of physical (embodied) service in case of an OR and 20 years for an officer. In the past, when TA concept of two months embodiment was being strictly followed, very few people could qualify for pension. But of late, more and more TA units are being embodied for prolonged periods and pension liability is on the rise. It must be appreciated that TA is a part-time concept and must retain its true nature. If employment requirements are more and embodiment of TA units is unavoidable in present circumstances, it is better to raise more TA units and embody them scarcely than to embody limited units for prolonged periods and let their personnel qualify for pension. This will be in both, national and conceptual interest. The costs saved could be utilized for enhancing the quality of equipment profile and training-infrastructure required for army. Also, prolonged embodiments are detrimental on two other accounts; firstly, all those who actually want to serve full time at the time of war and part time during peace are dissuaded; and secondly, the nation which despite having given a clear mandate of two month engagement to be followed to make it a low cost force, is cheated by making vast majority of TA cadres liable for pension. The cost difference in RA and TA unit is given below in a table.

COST COMPARISON

TYPE OF UNIT	RAISING COST (in crores)	RECURRING COST (in crores)
REGULAR ARMY STD INF BN	56	36
TA INF BN (Fully Embodied)	42	30
TA INF BN (Disembodied)	15	07

An example based on one person has been taken in the following table to show the difference in expenditure when TA concept is followed in its true spirit.

COST INCURRED ON ONE PERSON
SERVED FOR 20 YEARS IN TA

ITEM	WHEN TA CONCEPT FOLLOWED	WHEN TA CONCEPT NOT FOLLOWED
SALARY	40x24000=9.60,00 =10L	240x24000=57,60,000 =58L
PENSION (Considering individual retires at 45 and lives till 70 years)	NIL	25x12x10,000=30L
FAMILY PENSION (Considering wife lives for another 10 years)	NIL	10x12x5,000=06L
TOTAL PENSION LIABILITY	NIL	36L

NOTE – 80%TA(28,000 personnel) embodied for long time – likely to qualify for pension on completing 15 years physical service. Even if 50% qualify for pension, cost @36L will be 5040 crores. This amount is sufficient to raise **100 TA Battalions** that can be sustained for **FIVE years** on TA concept.

Weekend Concept of Training

As mentioned earlier, Provincial component of TA was bisected into Urban TA units and Provincial TA units after Shea Committee recommendations in 1924. This was very deliberate decision aimed at giving representation to urban masses as their occupations would not permit them an annual absence of over two months for joining provincial type of units. The training schedule in urban TA units is more appropriate for volunteers having busy civil jobs. Here, every volunteer who enrolls himself needs to come to his unit for 32 weekends (based on individual's choice) and for two weeks training camp in a year. This easy option enables many enthusiasts to enroll and offer their services to the national security.

As India is progressively becoming more and more urbanized, the increase in urban type of TA battalions will be justified. The present number of such units in TA is reduced to merely three - one in Delhi and two in Kolkata. This does not provide ample opportunity to aspirants belonging to other metros and fast growing urban areas. Another issue that needs to be kept in mind while raising such units is the willingness of employers of aspirants to spare them for war time or other grave national emergencies.

TA as a Relevant Tool for Social Integration

Today, when there is an unusual unrest in the civil society due to economic evolution and resultant enhanced aspirations of the people, the one organization that stands rock hard amidst all this confusion is, Armed Forces of the country. This may be due to its well defined organisational, social and professional parameters. Besides, people realize that it represents the whole country without any prejudice. There is space within it for each eligible member of the society. This uniqueness in its character makes it one of the most secular and functional organisations in the country. People look up to Armed

Forces with faith and hope to deliver at critical junctures. Since each member in armed forces is socially connected to the society, he/she is able to influence fellow citizens by merely being in Forces. Regular defence personnel, retired personnel and their relatives are, in a way, part of an extended family. This family is further enlarged when an opportunity to citizens, by way of part-time enrolment in armed forces, is offered. TA is called 'Citizens' Army' and people engaged in various civil professions join this force as part-timers. They come from various departments and spheres of society to fulfill their dream of serving the country as soldiers. Thus, they, in addition to influencing their homes and close relatives, also impact on their departments and peer groups they are working and interacting with in civil society. In a way, TA cadres are trained, responsible, disciplined and physically fit representatives of army in the civil society acting as a strong link between people and army. By bringing army closer to people of society, the aim is not at all to dream about a militarized society, but the endeavour is to inculcate characteristic ethos and strong points of army into citizens which will be useful in any stream of their lives as also for the defence of the country during emergencies. It does not require any survey to reveal that members of TA who have their businesses and vocations outside in civil, are doing extremely well. They do not hesitate in attributing their success to their army way of thinking and executing things. The big contribution that the TA can ensure towards society is to at least make everyone aware that such an organization where people can join defence forces voluntarily as part-timers exists in our country. India is full of people who do not want armed forces as a full time career but wish to contribute their bit during emergencies. To this end, already enrolled TA personnel spread a message in their spheres of influence. If TA has its footprint in all parts of the country, this will ensure uniform contribution from citizens in the defence set up of the nation and will further enhance social integration.

There is no denying the fact that, today, industry and civil corporates prefer more of their leaders from Services background. This is because; the selection system of officers (leaders) in Indian defence forces is one of the best in the world. Any employee in a civil company feels privileged to have passed Service Selection

Board (SSB) on joining TA and has a different sort of confidence all through his life. Industry and corporate world is realizing this fact and showing keen interest in TA concept. It is true that some ambiguities have crept into the system as regards employment of TA cadres and therefore, civil employers are wary of their employees being permanently taken away from them on their enrolment into TA. All such pin pricks will be adequately addressed in subsequent chapters by suggesting suitable remedial measures. One very important point has already been suggested by way of having more Urban TA units and strengthening weekend concept of training which does not impinge either employer or employee.

Progress on Various TA Review Committee Reports

A total of three review committees were constituted to evaluate TA since its inception but none of them has been taken seriously by the government. The last TA Review Committee Report of 1995 was submitted under the Chairmanship of Brig (Retd) K P Singh Deo. The committee was special because firstly, it was chaired by a Terrier who was a sitting Member of Parliament and Minister in Central Government; and secondly, it consisted of members from both Government and Services. This report gave valuable recommendations on expansion of TA and outlined a broad plan as to how TA should look like in future. This report was adopted by the Government and 'in principle' approval was given in 2002. However, very little progress could be made on ground because of difference in perception at the levels of MoD and Services HQ on many issues. This was evident when proposals were progressed on case to case basis for approval. Later, some internal studies were also ordered at Army HQ level on the subject but they turned out to be more of academic interest and nothing worthwhile came out of them for implementation.

CHAPTER IV

BENEFITS OF TERRITORIAL ARMY

"We cannot afford to pay taxes to maintain as large a standing army as we really require. The way for the nation to reduce the burden of taxation for defence purposes is to enlist and accept the apparent sacrifices involved in enlistment in the zonal Terrier Force. It is not really a sacrifice. In the result it will be found to be a gain to the individual who enlists. Lazy men who abhor or look down upon manual labour or who cannot fraternize with all classes of people, have no place in the Territorial Army."

- C Rajagopalachari

An All Inclusive Force

Benefits of any organization can be truly gauged by its short term as well as long term impact on the society. Since independence, the TA in its new form has consistently evolved and has come a long way. It has been able to leave an optimistic imprint on the psyche of our citizens through its selfless devotion to duty both in war and peace. Within the TA, there is a unit for everyone's choosing. This is a unique organization which has various types of units in its fold. These include; Infantry, Ecological, General Hospital, Oil Sector (ONGC & IOCL) and Railway Engineer units[1] . Some of these units though do not directly influence the battle field but are responsible to ensure different types of security like energy security, social security and environmental security in the country.

---

[1] Citizens' Army; a Coffee Table Book on TA by Additional Directorate General TA.

TA Personnel of Railway TA Unit

TA as part of Army has an inherent ability to augment its effect. The commonality of ethos and organization ensures its rapid and seamless integration with the Army. It has the ability to muster up its dormant resources to full effect within acceptable time line of the Army. This has been proved in all operations where TA participated since inception. It is one medium by which defence forces have been able to create closer association with the community. It provides platform to almost all types of people in the society to express their desire to serve the motherland in uniform as part-timers.

Today, the country has numerous organisations dealing with security related issues, functioning under different ministries and state governments. Each one of these wants to be independent in functioning and accounting. This has led to air-tight compartmentalization of resources, efforts and execution. It is possible that for the same task, more than one agency might be working without knowing each other's domain. More importantly, even if they know about each other, no coordination will be endeavoured towards effort and intelligence sharing. In this backdrop, it is becoming extremely difficult to maintain professional secularism amongst the agencies involved.

TA versus Para-Military and State Police Battalions

TA is an adjunct of Army and forms part of General Mobilisation Matrix. TA units are extensions of their regiments with flexible training and employment schedules suiting their members. Each TA unit belongs to a particular regiment and hence inherits the ethos, professional ethics and pride of that regiment. This becomes an identity and hallmark of unit personnel for rest of their lives. In TA, as the enrolment is zonal based, the manpower in a particular unit is more cohesive due to common regional bonds; unlike para-military battalions where cadres are drawn on all India basis. The enmeshing of TA units with regular army units, both during national emergencies and war is seamless as compared to para-military or state police units. This is because TA has common command and control structure as of Army and has regular army element in each TA unit as nucleus. In addition, embodiment and process of coming under command army in affected areas, is much faster in case of TA units as compared to para-military or state police units, they being under different ministries and states. But, the fundamental question that comes to mind is when the strength of Para Military Forces has increased manifold in past years and has reached over 13 lakhs, why Army and TA have still not been relieved to train for their own tasks? If, army is so badly required, why has it not been expanded for making the job easier for itself? After all, the money is going out of the same source. At the moment it looks as if armed forces and para military forces are functioning for the same cause but in divorced manner. The best bet would have been balanced expansion of TA based on zonal recruitment. It would have reserved the option of down scaling the strength by disembodying its manpower on situation getting improved. With the raising of more and more regular battalions of para military forces, this option is not there with the government.

Tangible Benefits

The presence of TA in the country gives an inclusive look to its defence forces. It provides to the citizens an opening to be a part of noble profession of arms dedicated to the defence of the country. The tangible benefits of TA are:-

(a) Cost Effectiveness. The security of the country cannot be compromised with budgetary obstacles and lack of resources. However, the wisdom lies in making judicious use of existing resources. The effect of the budget earmarked for defence can be enhanced by planned spending on human resource and infrastructure. TA units provide all these advantages to the nation. The annual recurring expenditure on manpower in a TA unit of matching strength is one sixth of what is expended on a regular unit. The training infrastructure required at any point and time in the unit is for only one sixth of the strength. In addition, the pension liability is negligible if the TA concept is truly followed.

(b) National Reserve. TA is trained manpower readily available for any eventuality. Barring few states in the country, TA has its presence across the country including Andaman & Nicobar Islands. This resource acts as an uncommitted reserve at the disposal of the nation during peacetime.

(c) Standing Army can be Made Lighter. The flexible characteristic of TA enables the country to raise regular units based on existing TA units if situation so demands; this was done post 1971 war. Conversely, if things are going smooth for the nation, identified trades and grades of the regular army can be TA-ised thereby saving money to the exchequer.

(d) Gainful Employment to People in Border Areas. The Home & Hearth battalions which have been raised in disturbed states, generated unprecedented goodwill among the common masses. Since the enrolment in these battalions is specific to states, the people have got employment at their door steps. This has raised their incomes and standard of living. The experiment has been very successful in bringing strayed youth back into national mainstream.

(e) Taking over Rear Area Security Duties during War. One of the tasks of TA is to relieve regular army of static duties for combat tasks. This ensures enhanced operational punch of regular army in battle front and committed security of rear areas by TA.

(f)   Contribution in War/ Counter Insurgency. Majority of infantry TA units are presently committed in insurgency related environment. The results produced by these units in the backdrop of terror threats have been praise worthy.

(g)   Use of Specialists. Today, there is no opening in the army to recruit or utilize services of specialists qualified in space, cyber space and other ultra-technical fields. It is increasingly becoming clearer that future warfare will be technology intensive where attacks would be planned on your information, decision making and economic centres. TA is flexible enough to have units of such specialists who can start streamlining counter measures while being on army's rolls.

(h)   Aid to Civil Authorities. Since TA units have their permanent earmarked locations, state governments invariably bank on them for any help during crisis. It is a normal practice to contact TA units during any disaster, floods and other unforeseen emergencies. During the times of Mr Rajiv Gandhi as Prime Minister of the country, there was a famine like situation in one of the states. Things were so bad that there was not enough manpower to distribute food grains released by the central government. This was the time when on the initiative of Brig (Retd) KP Singh Deo, a dedicated Terrier himself and the Minister at the Centre, TA was embodied and its services were taken for efficient distribution of food grains.[2] There are so many other instances where TA units promptly and efficiently assisted the civil administration; the list of emergencies attended is quite exhaustive.

(j) Enhancing Green Cover. With the raising of Ecological Battalions (TA), a very old problem of uncontrolled deforestation causing environmental degradation has been addressed. Such battalions operating in   D e h r a d u n (Mussorie Hills), Delhi (Bhatti Mines) and Rajasthan (Ram Garh area) have especially contributed a lot in improving the green cover and local environment.

---

[2]   Informal discussion held with Brig (Retd) KP Singh Deo on 28 Mar 2012

Intangible Benefits

In addition to physical benefits that the TA accrues, there are numerous indirect benefits that it offers to the nation. These cannot be quantified but certainly have great role in nation building. Some of these are:-

(a) Better Citizen - Soldier Bonding in the Society. A common citizen of the society engaged in civil profession, feels part of national defence on getting an opportunity to serve in uniform. Training in the army and work ethos contributes in making him mentally and physically strong. With his association with forces, the entire family and locality of the volunteer gets associated with the defence set up of the country. This creates a very strong bonding between the army and society which in turn gives great strength to Army as an organisation.

(b) Security Consciousness amongst Civil Population. As more and more people join the Part-Time Force, they keep coming in rotation for their two month training and going back to their civil vocations. Due to their repeated training and interaction with members of civil society, they start exhibiting responsible behaviour as regards security related issues. This influences the society and brings in much required security consciousness in the civilian citizens.

(c) Meeting Aspirations of Citizens towards Nation. Youth, by virtue of its adventurous attitude always takes fancy for military way of life. Most of the citizens, who dream of a uniformed life, want to be part of their defence forces. TA provides an excellent platform to the populace to live their dreams. It gives easy and convenient training schedules which can suit the requirements of people.

(d) Flexibility and Economy. Besides being cost effective in real terms, TA is flexible in its employment and offers economy of time during national emergencies. Being zonal in approach, TA personnel are well versed with the local areas around where they might be mobilised during unforeseen disaster or calamity.

(e) Benefits to Donor Organisation. The civil organisations that spare manpower to be part of TA as part-timers, are benefitted by receiving back, physically fit, well trained and disciplined employees. These soldiers induce their positive outlook on others also and thus the efficiency of the donor organisation improves.

(f) Updated Intelligence even when Troops Disembodied. In TA units, when men are disembodied, they still continue to remain in touch with their units. Their just being out there in the society, helps units in keeping track of untoward incidents, presence of terrorists or any related developments that might cause conflict in the society. In J&K, men while on leave have been instrumental in making militants either getting killed or causing their surrenders.

(g) Environmental Up-gradation. Ecological (TA) Battalions which are commonly called as Ecological TA Task Forces (ETFs) are contributing a lot towards upgrading environmental standards. Time bound plantation and its preservation has shown remarkable improvement in the environment of areas entrusted to these Task Forces and many of these have received national and international recognition befitting their contribution in preservation of environment.

The benefits of TA can be further enhanced if the government of the country makes it mandatory for all central employees to serve the armed forces for 4-5 years after they are enrolled into their parent services. Alternatively, all candidates aspiring to join central government services as officers, should be selected after their school education aging between 18- 20 years and be given common military training for four years. Other streams of entry into central services may concurrently be kept open but with the advantage to people who join after school through military training route. The psychology and aptitude during the training period should be critically analysed and accordingly, army and civil streams be decided and suggested after four year training. The problem of class war between army and civil cadres which is a major defeating force in the present system can be addressed with this arrangement. Also, there is a need to reach out to big corporate houses in the country to contribute their bit in national defence by way of sparing their manpower. Incentives based on their participation in Citizens' Army can be spelt out. This will help overcoming shortage of officers and the age old complaint of talent not opting for armed forces. State governments can reap some other benefits of this vibrant organization by asking for raising of TA units in various fields suiting to their requirements. The type of TA units that can be thought about to address many social difficulties that the states are facing have been covered in Chapter VI and X of the book.

CHAPTER V

CITIZENS' ARMIES OF OTHER COUNTRIES : AN OVERVIEW AND ANALYSIS

"Never doubt that a small group of thoughtful, committed citizens can change the world; indeed, it's the only thing that ever has."

- Margaret Mead

Changing Focus on Security

The emergence of unipolar world compelled many nations to restructure their armed forces. Ever since the US has emerged as a lead player, there is check in polarization race. The erstwhile mistrust and hostile tendencies amongst rival nations, giving rise to sudden and volatile builds up leading to total wars or war like situations, may not be seen in near future. A trend is visible where countries are down sizing their regular standing armies and the reliance is shifting on to creating more reserves; which are both, cost effective and demonstrate better connect with the society. This is happening in UK as well as in US. Exhaustive studies were ordered by both governments to draw road maps for future expansion and employment of their reserves. The inference indicates the concern and timely efforts by respective governments towards redefining their country's defence. In both cases, the study teams involved, have maintained a fine balance between holdings of regular and reserve components of their armies. Implementations suggested are phased and have been staggered to avoid creation of vacuum at any point of time. There is no denying the fact that maintenance of reserves by any nation is purely based on its unique compulsions, yet some general perceptions regarding importance being given to employment of reserve forces is seen emerging from a broader study of countries like Israel, US and UK. A broad comparison of important 10 armies of the world has been made to see the emphasis these countries attach to their reserve forces and changing trends in their employment philosophy.

COMPARISON TABLE [1]

S No	Country	Strength Regular Forces	Reserve Component	Paramilitary	Total
1.	US	1,458,219	1,458,500	11,035	2,927,754
2.	UK	197,780	212,400	NIL	410,180
3.	Australia	57,500	25,000	NIL	82,500
4.	China	2,285,000	800,000 + **8-10 million Militia**	1,500,000	4,585,000
5.	Japan	230,300	41,800	12,250	284,350
6.	Pakistan	617,000	513,000	304,000	1,434,000
7.	Vietnam	455,000	5,000,000	40,000	5,495,000
8.	Israel	176,500	565,000	8,050	749,550
9.	France	352,771	70,300	46,390	469,461
10.	**INDIA**	**1,325,000**	**2,142,821**	**1,300,586**	**4,768,407**

United States of America

The US army has evolved to its present structure from colonial based militia force that came into being in 1638. It consists of three components - the Active Army, the Army Reserve and the Army National Guard. The National Guard of US is equivalent to the Territorial Army in India. The primary difference between National Guard and active duty army is the time spent working. The National Guard is component of army but not a full time job. The work requirements for National Guard are **one weekend per month, two weeks per year**[2]. The much awaited restructuring in the US army got underway after 9/11 terrorist attacks against the homeland of the US. These attacks; coupled with the increasingly big scaled natural disasters in recent years, confirmed that the US required military

---

[1] Mickopedia, the free encyclopedia

[2] Difference Between National Guard and Army by Michael Summers, eHow Contributor

forces that were readily available and which could quickly and successfully take appropriate action in support of defence, safety and welfare of the communities, states and of their country. According to a report from the US government accountability office, National Guard forces were considered well suited for civil support missions because of their locations across the country and experience in supporting neighbouring communities in times of crisis.[3]

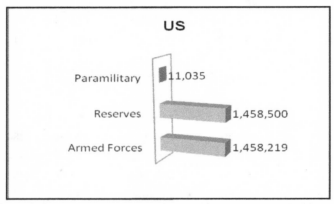

As regards the US reserve component (RC), it has over 14 lakh members and constitutes approximately half of total US force. It is thoroughly integrated with all US missions. National Guard (NG), one of the seven elements of Reserve Force, has 77% army component (Army National Guard – ARNG) and 23% air component (Air National Guard - ARN). National Guards are stationed in every State, Territory and District and operate under their State Governor or Territorial Adjutant General (TAG). They are organized as an operational force capable of accomplishing state, national and international missions during war and peace.

To effectively meet the above mentioned requirements, the ARNG adopts a homogeneous mix of Combat, Combat Support and Combat Service Support units. They are structured to integrate seamlessly with Active Component units as and when required. Units of ARNG are located in nearly 3,000 communities throughout the United States enabling them to respond rapidly to domestic emergencies.

[3]   The US Govt Accountability Office. Statement of David M Walker, Comptroller General of the US, 20 Oct 2005.

Role and Function of ARNG. The ARNG has a dual role of working as federal as well as state force. It is directly accessible to the National Command Authority and is responsive to state governors as well. Under its federal obligation, it supports US national security objectives by providing trained and equipped units for prompt mobilization in the event of national emergency or war. In its state functions, it protects life, property, peace, order and public safety in the society.

The current strength of ARNG is about 350,000 in the Selected Reserve, which is almost 33 percent of regular army. It consists of eight divisions and 34 brigade combat teams (BCT). The Army National Guard is currently reorganizing into 28 brigade combat teams (reduced from 32) and 78 support brigades as a part of the Army's transformation plan. On completion of transformation, each brigade will have 3,000 to 4,000 soldiers.[4] The new arrangement is being termed as modular design.[5] ARNG is unique in its employment and its components can be used in one of the three legally distinct ways:

- By the Governor for a state purpose authorized by state law.

- By the Governor, with the concurrence of the President, for a shared state/federal purposes.

- By the President for a federal purpose authorized by federal law.

United Kingdom

The British ground forces have been resorting to the use of volunteers for hundreds of years during times of crisis. The first such unit of volunteers is believed to have been raised in 1537[6].Volunteer units were raised in view of perceived threats when regular forces required assistance. Most of these units used to be of infantry, artillery and yeomanry. Yeomanry units consisted of gentlemen farmers and tenants and were mounted in nature. In 1907 Parliament passed legislation by which the consolidation of the yeomanry and volunteers into

---

[4] Army National Guard – Wikipedia, the free encyclopedia.

[5] USAWC Strategy Research Project of 2006 by Lt Col Michael J. Garshak

[6] Territorial Army (TA) : www.globalsecurity.org/militias/world/india/ta.htm

Territorial Force was done. The first new unit was raised on 01 Apr 1908, and this day is taken as the birth of present Territorial Army (TA) in UK. The units of this force were mobilized in 1914 till 1918, and on their demobilization, were disbanded only to be re-raised in 1920 as part-time Territorial Army units[7]. The strength of this force expanded to nearly two lakh during WWII.

Till mid-1990s, the TA saw ups and downs with a fluctuating fortune. The TA during this period was never regarded as a particularly useable or effective force both by the government of the day and the country's regular army. In the later years of 1990s and the turn of the millennium, British regular army got increasingly engaged in overseas operations and this saw the TA assume a more high profile and well defined role. It moved from being termed as 'a force of last resort' to 'reserve of first choice' in supporting the regulars. The TA is the largest of all other reserve forces named, Royal Naval Reserve (RNR), the Royal Marines Reserve (RMR) and the Royal Air Force Volunteer Reserve (RAFVR). The TA is divided into three types of unit; National, Regional and Sponsored. While joining, the volunteer has a choice of at least two types of unit, depending on how far he is prepared to travel for training.

The TA in UK occupies approximately 380 sites spread across the country. There is a thought process underway to rationalize these sites and cover new populous areas that do not have TA centres.

Role of UK TA. As per UK government review of armed forces[8], TA has two important roles as given below:-

- To provide highly trained soldiers who can work alongside the regulars on missions in the UK and overseas.

- To give people with specialist skills, like medics and engineers, a range of exciting opportunities to use them in new ways.

Australia

Australia's military history began with the formation of part time

---

[7]   British Army Website.

[8]   British Army Website.

military units. The first such part-time defence units were raised in Sep 1800. Known as the Sydney and Parramatta Loyal Associations, they were raised in response to fears of Irish and convict uprisings and, later, to the possibility of French raids during the Napoleonic Wars. The troops of these units were not to expect pay for the volunteer offer of their services. They were to assist British troops in suppressing local rebellions and carried on with this role till 1810 when they were disbanded as British troops arrived to deal with the defence of Australia. This carried on till 1870. However, from 1854, British forces were supported by volunteer part-time forces raised in each of the colonies (States).[9]

The present structure of Australian land forces contains two components- **Australian Regular Army (ARA)** and **Australian Army Reserve (AAR).** The Reserve Component (AAR) has two type of forces under it as, **Standby Reserve** and **Active Reserve.** Active Reserve has further sub- sub components as **High Readiness Reserve** and **Reserve Response Force** under it. These components are basically categories of service, which are determined by the level of training obligation and a commitment that a member is required to meet. The present strength of Australian reserve forces is approximately 30,000.[10]

Role of AAR. The role of AAR encompasses the '3Rs',

- Reinforcement.

- Round Out.

- Rotation.

The part-time reserve forces of Australia are free to be deployed in other countries for the above mentioned tasks, unlike earlier times when their deployment used to be restricted within the homeland.

China

In China, the part-time service concept is followed in the Reserve component of PRC's armed forces, called the Reserve Force. The first

9   Red Coats to Cams- Australia's Volunteer Part- Time Military Forces by Matt Walsh.

10   Australian Military Forces – Wikipedia, the free Encyclopedia.

reserve force was created in 1955 but was disbanded in 1957. The present reserve force of PLA was created in 1983. The 1984 Military Service Law stipulated the combination of the militia and the reserve service system. The reserve force in China has undergone radical reforms in structure and mission since 1998. It was during the 1999 National Day military parade held in Beijing that their reserve force appeared for the first time as one of the parade formations.

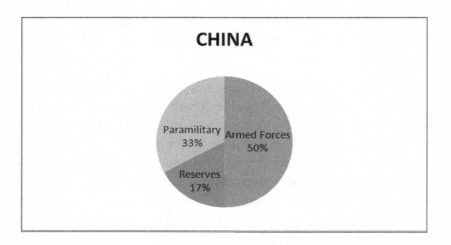

The reserve force is composed of part-time reserve soldiers, mostly militia and demobilized soldiers, as well as reserve service officers. The PLA reservists are organized into reserve divisions, brigades and regiments which are subordinate to various military district headquarters. Army reserve units are estimated to include tank, infantry, artillery, anti-air craft artillery (AAA), surface to air missile, engineering, signal, pontoon bridge, chemical defence and logistics support units.[11] Reserve infantry divisions are generally found in every province and autonomous region. Since 1999, each military region has established a reserve logistics support brigade to sustain reserve and active duty operations. Many soldiers in the PLA reserve force are ex active army personnel but many units recruit specialized civilians without prior services background to fill specific technical needs.[12] The present strength of PLA reserve force is:-

---

[11] Army Reserve – SinoDefence.com, 10 Jul 2012.

[12] Chinese Army Modernization: An Overview by Lt Col Dennis J Blasko, US Army, Retired.

- PLA Reserve   -   800,000

- Militia   -   8 - 10 million[13]

Role. The reserve force implements orders and regulations of the PLA and is incorporated into the PLA's order of battle. In peacetime, the reserve force units are led by the provincial military districts or garrison commands and can be employed for maintaining social order in accordance with the law, and in wartime, after mobilization, they are commanded by the active units for either augmenting active forces or operate independently as local defence forces.[14]

Japan

The Imperial Japanese Army (IJA) was the official ground based armed force of the Empire of Japan, from 1871 to 1945, till it was defeated in WW II. At its peak, the IJA had 6,095,000 men on rolls. After WW II, the Allied occupation authorities were committed to the demilitarization and democratization of Japan. All clubs, schools and societies associated with the military, and martial skills were eliminated. The general staff was abolished along with army, navy ministries, the Imperial Army and Imperial Navy. Article 9 of the constitution of Japan, adopted on November 3, 1946, explicitly bans the creation of armed forces. However, over the past fifty years, Japan has built up land, air and sea-based Self-Defence Forces (SDF) to protect the country in case of attack. In recent years, the Japanese Government has passed law to extend the SDF beyond Japan to other countries[15].

The SDF is a unique military system where all personnel are technically civilians; those in uniform are classified as special civil servants and are subordinate to the ordinary civil servants who run the Ministry of Defence. There are no military secrets or military laws. Each unit of the force has an element of reserves (part-time) on its establishment who are called as on required basis. The total reserve component in the force is 41,800. The Army Reserve has two reserve

---

[13] Chinese Military Overview – SinoDefence.com, 18 May 2012.

[14] GlobalSecurity.org: PLA Reserve Forces.

[15] Japan's About-Face, Wideangle, July 8th, 2008.

components – the rapid reaction reserve component and the main reserve component. The members of rapid-reaction component train 30 days a year and that of main reserve train five days a year. As per the terms of Mutual Security Assistance Pact, ratified in 1952 and the peace treaty Japan had signed with the US and other countries, the role spelt out for Japan's forces (both ground and maritime) was only to deal with internal threats and natural disasters; this continues to be the same even now, for all practical purposes. However, as per new laws, SDF is being used for following tasks in other countries:-

- Peacekeeping and International disaster relief operations under the International Peace Cooperation Law.

- SDF deployments under the Anti-Terrorism Special Measures Law[16].

Pakistan

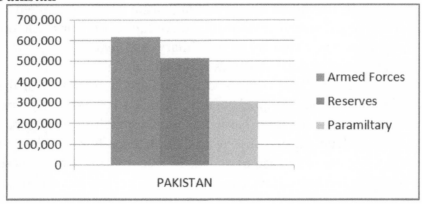

The Reserve Force (**the National Guard**) of Pakistan is one of the three components of its Paramilitary Forces; the other two being, the Armed Security Forces (the Rangers and Frontier Corps) and the Maritime Security Agency. Pakistan National Guard comprises the Mujahid Force, the Janbaz Force and locally recruited militia. Also included to this, are the **National Cadet Corps** and the **Women's Guard**.[17] As per the report of Institute of Peace and Conflict Studies

---

[16] Japan's About-Face, Wideangle, July 8th, 2008.

[17] Paramilitary Forces of Pakistan – Wikipedia, the free encyclopedia.

(IPCS) New Delhi and figures given out by Wikipedia, the strength of Pakistan National Guard (out of total paramilitary strength of 427,627), is 185,000. Compared to regular army, this roughly works out to **23 percent**.[18]

The Pakistan National Guard consists of 79 battalions including six artillery and five training battalions. Many of these battalions are on permanent embodiment. Training battalions are primarily meant to provide training to disembodied battalions. In addition, the field formations of the army are also tasked to give training. National Guard units participate in collective training with their regular army. The recruitment is generally done from local areas and people within age limit of 18 to 30 years (45 years for ex-servicemen) can join. Janbaz Force units, though part of National Guards, operate under respective provincial governments during peacetime.

Role. Other than being used for training, internal threats and disaster management related tasks during peacetime; the Pakistan National Guard is used in combat role in defensive operations during war. In addition, units of this force are engaged for providing reinforcements to rear area security and guarding vulnerable points by way of light air defence capability during war.[19]

Vietnam

The Vietnam People's Army (VPA) was founded in Dec 1944. This army is a "Triple Armed Force" composed of the Main Force, the Local Force and the Border Force. Like many other countries' armed forces, the VPA consists of standing or regular forces as well as reserve forces. During peacetime, the standing forces are minimized in number and kept combat-ready by regular physical and weapons training, and stock maintenance. Reserves exist in all service branches and are organized in same way as the standing forces, with the same chain of command, and with officers and non-commissioned officers.

The part-time element in Vietnam's army is seen in its militia component of Local Forces. Local forces are an entity of the VPA that together with the militia and 'self defence forces', act on the local

---

[18] UNHCR/ Refworld, the Leader in Refugee Decision Support.

[19] Pakistan Army Information.

level in protection of people and local authorities. The militia consists of rural civilians; and the self defence forces consist of civilians who live in urban areas and/or work in large groups, such as construction sites or farms. The militia and self defence force is a part-time force of the masses. The current number stands at 3-4 million part-time soldiers.[20]

Israel

The evolution of present Israel Defence Forces (IDF) is very interesting and motivating. The current structure of high technology-driven IDF is based on the solid foundation laid by handful of volunteer soldier-farmers during the fight for Jewish independence in the land of Israel in 1940s. The founders of IDF have made extreme sacrifices until 1950s in keeping this force alive. The senior commanders who were generally very young in age, did not earn wages and live by growing their own food.

Israel has a system whereby most citizens have to serve IDF for a period ranging from two to three years. The military service is obligatory for both sexes; only selected few are exempted. All eligible men and women are drafted at the age of 18 and continuously serve for 36 months and 21 months respectively. On completion of this obligatory period, each soldier is assigned a reserve unit. Men are maintained as reserves till 45 years of age and during this time they are called for refresher training for 39 days every year.

The concept of part-time service in Israel is practiced by the soldiers once they are placed on reserve list and become part of reserve units. These soldiers keep working in their respective civil professions and also keep pursuing their military career as part timers. The actual location, identity and strength of IDF is not disclosed by the government, however, as per the estimates made by the International Institute for Strategic Studies in London of 2004, the strength of Israel ground forces stood at 125,000 troops, including 40,000 career soldiers and 85,000 conscripts, with an additional 600,000 men and women in the reserves. There, however, were plans in IDF to cut down the ground forces by about 20 percent over five years period

---

[20] Vietnam People's Army – Wikipedia, the free encyclopedia.

starting 2003. The IDF reserve battalions constitute 70 percent of the combatants. They constitute backbone of the army. It is common in Israel to see two generations serving simultaneously in the army – the son doing obligatory service and father in reserves.

Role. The original role thought for the reserves in 1950s was to serve as the principal fighting force at the times of war. But with the passage of time, there came changes and at present, about 80 percent of reserve duties are devoted to maintenance and administration operational work not directly connected to combat. This change in approach is a result of the IDF not having to pay the real cost of its reserve forces.[21]

France

The military history of France is over 2000 years old. The present French Armed Forces have a reported strength of 3.52 lakh including over one lakh Gendarmerie (a force meant to enforce law in society). In addition, they have approximately 70,000 reserves. On the suspension of obligatory national service and the professionalization of the army in 2006, France also modified the organization of its military reserve. The military reserve was organized into two bodies:

- **Citizen Reserve** - group of volunteers actively getting to know the military world, undergoing training maintaining the links between the armed forces and the civil society. These reservists have military status.

- **Operational Reserve** – grouping together reservists with an ESR (obligation to serve in the reserve) and former military officers with an availability obligation. The reservists serving under an ESR serve as military officers for periods of 1 to 210 days per year and come from all fields and all professional social categories. These reservists serve in many branches of the forces – the air force, army, gendarmerie, navy, health service and supply.[22]

Role. The role assigned to French military reserve as per law enacted

---

[21] GlobalSecurity.org – Army-Israel.

[22] Military Reserve Forces of France – Wikipedia, the free encyclopedia.

in 1999[23] is:

- Augmentation of armed forces.

- Connecting the armed forces with the nation.

- Maintaining the spirit of defence.

Inference

The study of part-time forces of various countries reveals the different requirements of each nation. It is seen that the concept is dynamic and ever evolving. No particular part-time service model may be perfect in functioning, but with continuous innovations based on functional requirements, **part-time concept** in armed forces can be redefined and go a long way in keeping any nation ready for unforeseen eventualities.

Considering requirements of India, the existing part-time reserve force (TA) can be suitably modified and made much more effective. Some of the changes that can be incorporated into the present structure should include; clear defining of various components of TA based on its requirement, availability of manpower and its pragmatic employment. This should be ably supported by modified training for each component. To achieve that, the component having direct access to common citizens of the society (Non-departmental TA) should have two clear categories as follows:-

- Active TA.

- Reserve TA.

At the time of commissioning/enrolment only, the candidates have to choose either of the above mentioned two categories. There should, however, be a provision which enables personnel of Reserve TA to switch over to Active TA if they wish to. Requisite training should be mandatory for absorption in Active TA.

Active TA

This will further have two sub-categories as **Combat TA** and **Combat Support TA**. The Combat TA will include TA units of infantry and

---

[23] Military Reserve Forces of France – Wikipedia, the free encyclopedia.

TA regiments of armour and artillery which are planned for holding formations (covered in Chapter VIII). Their role and equipment profile needs to be accordingly modified. The Combat Support TA will include H&H TA units for providing assistance to army in CI operations and while extending aid to civil authorities. During war, this TA will continue to follow its existing role and task in forward and depth areas.

Reserve TA

Reserve TA will include all units raised on Urban concept. In addition, all ecological TA battalions; which presently fall under Departmental category, should also be part of Reserve TA; as manpower of these units is ex-army and do not belong to any civil department. They, thus, do not qualify to be called Departmental Units. The role and task of reserve TA units should also continue as hitherto fore.

Proposed Training and Service Liability for Active TA Personnel

- **Other Rank (OR)**
    - Post Enrolment Training (Recruit Training) - Nine months (one month at Unit level prior to eight months at Regimental Centre).
    - Liability of Service - Minimum two months in a year.
- **Officers**
    - Pre-Training - One month at TA Training School Deolali.
    - Post Commission Training - Three months at IMA.
    - Liability of Service - Minimum two months in a year.

Proposed Training and Service Liability for Reserve TA Personnel

- **Other Rank (OR)**
    - Post Enrolment Training (Recruit Training) - One month at unit level.
    - Liability of Service - 32 Weekends in a year and 14 Days Annual Training Camp.

- **Officers**

  - Post Commission Training - One month at TA Training School, Deolali.

  - Liability of Service - 32 Weekends training in a year and 14 Days Annual Training Camp.

CHAPTER VI

CONCEPT OF HOME AND HEARTH AND ITS FUTURE RELEVANCE

"War can only be abolished through war, and in order to get rid of the gun it is necessary to take up the gun."

- Mao Zedong

Genesis of Home and Hearth

It is an observed phenomenon that living beings defend themselves in most furious manner when their homes and off springs are threatened. In humans also, the survival instinct is on its peak when their kith and kin, community, clan and living boundaries are affected. This unique characteristic of human behaviour had been the basis of social defence in societies of yester years. In the past, all members of the community, irrespective of their professional disposition, would get together and collectively fight against any external assault. The raising of Home and Hearth (H&H) TA units was probably conceptualized keeping this aspect of human nature in mind. The fact followed is, 'no one else can defend your home and hearth better than you yourself.' This philosophy is based on, 'Sons of Soil' concept where people are recruited on regional basis; trained and used for the defence of same area they belong to. They themselves are the intelligence mechanism, interpreters and tacticians to work out suitable strategies for defence of the area; of course, in collaboration with other existing agencies.

The idea of raising an army of local people was conceived by some enlightened members of parliament in 2002 during discussion on national security. The Ministry of Defence (MoD), thereafter pursued the idea and took it to its logical conclusion. All formalities at Government level were over by end 2003 and raising of first set of H&H TA battalions commenced 2004 onwards.

In any society, one of the primary reasons of its masses getting alienated from the mainstream is economic disparity. This factor brings in a sense of frustration and rebellion amongst the educated youth who then fall prey to divisive elements and start working against the national interest. Once triggered, this is extremely difficult to arrest. India being a very large country with varied terrains, climate, cultures and demography has had its share of problems that any evolving democracy has during its early years. The uneven and asymmetric distribution of funds for developmental activities in the country gave the people an instrument to agitate and take the law in their own hands to follow the path of destruction. The idea of raising H&H TA battalions is a step to arrest this erosion in the society. It is focused on raising units with manpower recruited and drawn from hitherto neglected local border areas with the aim of, firstly, reducing response time for mobilization, defending their own home and hearth, keeping vigil along the border and gaining field intelligence even when troops remained in disembodied state; and secondly, helping create suitable conditions for providing a source of occupation, thereby generating income to the locals of these areas.[1] These units were initially intended to be raised for Northern and North-Eastern borders of the country. The concept can be extended to other remote tribal areas where problem of local youth becoming anti-national is on the rise. An agreement is learnt to be afloat between Ministry of Defence (MoD) and Ministry of Home Affairs (MHA) to raise H&H TA battalion consisting of local tribal youth in Maoist affected areas. MHA wants MoD to raise minimum three battalions one each for Chhattisgarh, Jharkhand and Odisha.[2]

Alongside H&H TA units, another very adventurous and challenging experiment of raising a TA battalion constituting surrendered terrorists was also tried in the northern state of J&K in 2004-05. The recruitment procedure for this unit was similar to that of a H&H TA battalion. The initial apprehensions about its success

---

[1]   The Citizens' Army – Coffee Table Book on Territorial Army.

[2]   DNA – India, Sunday, Mar 12, 2012; 'To Beat Maoists, Centre Plans an Army of Tribals'.

were soon reversed when the unit started giving intangible results. The idea of this experiment was twofold; firstly, to bring back estranged nationals into the main stream treating them at par with all citizens of the country; and secondly, to include them as part of the national security mechanism to make them feel as responsible part of the nation.

Performance Appraisal of Home and Hearth TA Units

Under the concept of 'Home and Hearth', a few TA battalions that are raised to cover border areas have been a success in not only security related tasks but also in social and economic development of the border areas. In a very short span of 5-7 years of their existence, these battalions have created a mark in the society and local people have started identifying themselves with these units. These battalions are deemed to have been a greater success particularly in Jammu & Kashmir. The success of these battalions can be gauged from the fact that today, any regular army formation operating in counter insurgency areas in Jammu & Kashmir or Northeastern states, vehemently asks for H&H TA troops for providing intelligence and information on the local terrain. Another advantage that is envisaged of these units is the continuous inflow of intelligence even when troops are on leave or disembodiment. The TA unit composed of surrendered terrorists, commonly called *Ikhwanis* belonging to the local areas of Kashmir Valley, has been able to eliminate over 300 terrorists since its inception. The record of other H&H TA battalions in this regard has also been well above the other units. The figures are respectable and comparable with the results produced by regular army units. The army has acknowledged the valour and contribution of the *Ikhwanis* and other H&H troops with military decorations.[3]

Implications of Home and Hearth Units

Any Territorial Army battalion has an element of permanent staff in it which is partly contributed by the parent Regiment of that battalion. At the time of raising of a TA unit, some additional staff over and above the permanent element, is loaned from regular units for initial stabilisation of the unit. This is returned on the basis of sliding scale

---

[3] Indian Military Review, Jun 2011: Surrender, Amnesty and Rehabilitation in J&K, Benefits and Pitfalls by Jaibans Singh.

keeping in view the anticipated seniority and promotion achieved by the original cadres of the new unit. The educational qualification for TA recruit is 10+2 pass; similar to what is prevalent in regular army. However, this convention was not strictly followed in the case of H&H TA battalions and relaxation in education standards was given by the government to give representation to more people hailing from difficult border areas. As the mandate of H&H only permits recruitment of locals for its units, manpower from sister battalions of the Regiment could not be transferred in desired numbers while raising these units. As a result of this factor coupled with urgency of raising these units, almost complete manpower was freshly recruited as jawans. This has led to serious cadre management problems now. On one hand loaned personnel from regular army are due to be returned to donor units and on the other, there being less aspirants interested in passing promotion exams and making up the rank structure, a state of flux is being faced in some units. These are serious challenges and need to be addressed at the earliest.

The creation of H&H TA battalions has raised another very important issue regarding their embodiment mandate. Whereas in normal TA battalions, the concept of part-time is followed from the first year itself, for H&H TA battalions, five year continuous embodiment was given keeping in view the sensitivity in their native areas and areas of operation. Not only this, further extension was given for two to five years. Ever since their raising, these units have not been disembodied till now, and for this reason, they are more like regular units and less like TA. The troops and families of these units have started considering their job as a regular career. This has a serious implication. Based on two assumptions, it will be extremely difficult now to disembody personnel of these units hailing from sensitive areas. Firstly, there will always remain an element of doubt in Army's mind if some of these personnel could go to terrorists' fold if sent on disembodiment; which would eventually mean handing over trained soldiers to separatists on a platter. Secondly, as personnel of H&H TA battalions have never been disembodied so far, on coming to know of their disembodiment for the first time, local people may protest citing it as a government gimmick to terminate their children's services or avoid pension to their wards. This feeling could be further exploited by anti-national elements.

Another very important implication is following of the TA concept in H&H TA units. In India, the TA is already over stretched and the part-time concept is facing extreme challenges. There is an acute pressure from employers' side against army's prolonged embodiment requirements of their employees. By calling them for long embodiments, the part-time concept is being harmed and nation is not getting benefitted. Due to this, most of TA cadres, especially officers, have to quit either of their two jobs. This is sending a wrong message into the society. At present it looks as if the concept is sinking and that it needs immediate resuscitation. It is high time gradual disembodiment of these units is started; a coy each can be disembodied for one to two months in the first year and subsequently increased to the actual period. This will be in both, national and institutional interest.

As discussed earlier, one of the primary reasons for raising H&H TA battalions was providing employment to people of neglected border areas. If this logic remains the primary plank of social upliftment in such areas then disbandment of these battalions is unimaginable in foreseeable future even if ground situation in the area totally improves. In such a scenario, the best option would be to convert these units into regular battalions accepting exceptions of education and age. Alternatively, they are converted into TA battalions, allotted operational task and rotated all over the country during peace time like other TA units are made to do. As per present mandate, H&H TA battalions operate only in local areas where they have been raised. Keeping these units at same locations over protracted periods would invite indiscipline, corruption and, at times, willful vengeance in the society. This aspect needs deliberate analysis to avoid subsequent knee jerk reactions.

Future Employment of Home and Hearth Units

The 'Home and Hearth' is a unique concept and can be optimally utilized for varied national requirements. At present, H&H TA units are mostly operating in Counter Insurgency (CI) scenario. Their role and task has been clearly spelt out for both war and peace and is generally intelligence related. These units can be employed in some of the following additional tasks in future.

During War

The present role of H&H TA battalion during war is to execute Rear Area Security (RAS) tasks to include security and protection of lines of communication and VA/VPs.

In addition to existing role, H&H TA unit can be employed in further enhancing the efficiency of the organization by sparing regular combatants for operations. Some of the important tasks could include:

- Protection of Head Quarters in forward areas.
- Interpreters and guides during forward reconnaissance missions.
- Facilitators during evacuation of own villages.
- Part of convoy protection parties moving within battle areas.
- Co-drivers with forward moving convoy vehicles.
- Quick Reaction Teams at Tactical Head Quarters.
- Road Opening duties.

During Peace

At present the task of H&H TA battalion during peace is to assist regular army in protection of lines of communication in sensitive areas and help in counter terrorism/infiltration, reconnaissance, surveillance and intelligence collection. In addition, it also assists army to conduct military civic actions smoothly. Certain very important tasks can also be considered for TA within the society during peace times. These could be:-

- **Disaster Management Tasks.** H&H TA battalions can be suitably modified, equipped and trained for numerous important tasks for peace time employment. A very important task where suitably modified H&H battalions can be employed is in the field of 'disaster management'. Presently, there is a separate central authority- National Disaster Relief Authority (NDMA) in the country for disaster management. This has raised its separate Disaster Relief Task Forces for disaster related requirements. In fact, there is not at all a requirement of raising exclusive units for this task; existing H&H TA/ TA units can be prepared as dual task units for this. Each state as per its size and requirements can bid for one or two units (H&H or Infantry TA) to be raised in affected areas. These units can be embodied during required months as on required basis. It can be ensured that each such unit has an officer trained with NDMA who is the advisor to the CO on disaster related issues. The unit/companies when mobilized for disaster management task should work under the direction of NDMA. The monetary effects can be shared by both MoD and NDMA. Alternatively, another model wherein, 3-4 dedicated companies of H&H TA/TA unit in each state can be earmarked for disaster management duties working under the battalion CO and having NDMA's representatives in each such battalion. The provision of specialist equipment, training, embodiment and costing of these companies remains with NDMA. This arrangement will give pan India presence to NDMA as also an advantage of making use of existing infrastructure and working in close quarters with army.

- **Line of Control (LC) Fencing.** Another area where H&H battalions can be effectively employed is, the maintenance of barbed wire fencing at the LC. This is commonly called LC fencing and is an important annual requirement in the northern state of J&K. So far, whole/parts of Pioneer/ Engineer regiments are mobilized from far off places every year for the job. It would be beneficial in all respects if troops of H&H TA battalions are utilized for this task. They can be embodied after winter months to carry out necessary repairs of the damaged fence. These troops being from local areas will not require unnecessary movement and customary acclimatization etc. The savings in financial terms would be enormous. In addition to providing intelligence on the area, such units will also contribute immensely in infrastructural development of the area during their disembodied periods. If the state governments and industry players cooperate with MoD then the troops belonging to these units can be absorbed into state government departments or state industrial units as permanent employees during their disembodied period. Physically fit, disciplined and loyal men carrying army ethos of working will be available to them at no additional cost. In addition, this will also generate a very positive goodwill for the governments of the states.

- **Ecology Tasks.** At present some states have Ecological Task Forces of TA working on various ecological projects within state boundaries. This effort has been appreciated world over. These task forces are based on ex- servicemen of respective states who are committed to improve the ecology of their areas. Like these task forces, H&H TA units can also be used by the states; in consultation with central government, to arrest environmental degradation of their areas. If state governments are ready to contribute financially, H&H TA troops can be embodied for 2-3 months in a year for enhancing and maintaining the green cover of the region; working closely with state forest departments. These troops can be embodied as on required basis and during this period, creation of check dams, ponds, irrigation channels etc can be planned. Besides, existing green cover and newly created infrastructure can also be maintained by making use of these trained troops.

- **Vocational Training.** H&H TA units are ideally suited for bringing in much desired financial freedom among the masses of the remote areas they are raised in. State governments with the help of corporate world and industry can make use of manpower and expertise of these units in running small scale industrial units for the villagers. These units can act as training hubs for imparting vocational technical training to aspiring boys and girls of the area. Each state can identify sustainable vocations and tailor-made training courses can be started based on the requirements of the people. This venture can bring in basic social change and will directly connect the army with the society.

- **Self Defence Training.** Another important aspect that needs attention in the society is, 'Self Defence'. The upkeep of spirit of self defence is a must among the people living in difficult areas. This can be one of the agenda for the future employment of H&H TA units. Since disembodied manpower of H&H TA units will be trained in their unit locations over the whole year, short training capsules on self/community/village defence can also be run for the local villagers in their free times. They can be trained to fight against robberies, earthquakes, fire-hazards and other man-made or natural disasters. Self defence is directly linked to civil defence. The importance that is given to civil defence in national security in the US has been very deliberately covered in 'Report on Civil Defence Planning in the United States of America' published in *Army Information Digest U.S.A.- Jan, 1949.*[4] The statement issued by Secretary Napolitano on 19 April, 2013 appreciating the efforts and contributions made by civil society in apprehending April 2013 Boston attackers is reproduced below:-

The apprehension of the suspect tonight is a significant development in the ongoing FBI-led investigation of the Boston bombings. I commend the federal, state and local law enforcement and first responders who have been and contribute to work tirelessly to get to the bottom of the senseless attacks in Boston, and defend and protect American public.

- **Specialists' Units.** The list of tasks for H&H TA can be endless. It is up to local governments to reap the benefits by making use of part-time soldiers present in a particular area by spending miniscule amounts (some percentage of MNAREGA funds) on their salaries. The concept of part-time soldiering is so unique that specialists from any field can be enrolled and can contribute in nation building. One of the finest examples to corroborate this fact can be the projects undertaken by **US National Guard Agriculture Development Teams (ADTs)** working in close quarters with provincial governments and local farmers of war torn Afghanistan. While operating in Afghanistan, the commanders of US army must have seen an immense scope for improvement in agriculture sector that was marred by mismanagement caused due to prolonged militancy. ADTs consisting of US agriculture specialists were

---

4   Military Digest, Issue Number 1, April 1949.

raised as a part of US National Guard (part-time force) and inducted into Afghanistan. This initiative has contributed a lot in improving agriculture skills of local farmers and enabling them in identifying suitable crops and methods of cultivation. Today, these teams have undertaken projects in, basic gardening practices, bee keeping, livestock production, large watershed and irrigation. President Obama says that US will enhance agriculture development instead of big reconstruction projects to build Afghanistan's economy, to have an immediate impact on Afghan people.[5]

Besides being an inherent reserve force at the disposal of the country and states, part-time force acts as a great economic savior. The best part about part-time force is its low liability factor. If at any point and time, it is felt that the mission for which a particular type of unit was raised has been accomplished, that unit can be disbanded. Also, chances of pension liability are minimal in such a force if troops are judiciously used as per concept. Eventually, it is always a 'win-win' situation for both society and the government. Creation of TA units based on H&H concept along border and other sensitive areas can be an excellent value addition for the nation. An extract taken out from the paper presented by Lt Gen (Retd) NS Narhari, PVSM at the inaugural seminar of Centre for Land Warfare Studies (CLAWS) held in Nov 2004 is reproduced below:-

It may not be cost effective to have a parallel force for CI operations and anti-terrorist operations. RR was created for this in the late 1980s. I believe there is some procedural problem in paramilitary forces working under RR formations. This should be solved at the Government of India level. The TA units raised initially as a second line of defence have not got the same statuary support as national guard units have in the US. TA battalions raised on regional basis and trained as army units can supplement forces for CI operations; they have been doing their bit now, including CI operations and disaster relief. Their mobilization time should be refined and supported by an Act of Parliament[6].

---

[5]   National Guard of the United States – Wikipedia, the free encyclopedia.

[6]   Army 2020 – Shape, Size, Structure and General Doctrine for Emerging Challenges, edited by Lt Gen (Retd) Vijay Oberoi, PVSM, AVSM, VSM.

CHAPTER VII

NEED FOR TERRITORIAL ARMY FOOTPRINT ACROSS THE COUNTRY

"To be prepared for war is one of the most effectual
means of preserving peace"

- George Washington

Indian States with Armed Forces Footprint

The constitution of India directs our Armed Forces to be apolitical guardians of the country; well above communal, regional and religious affiliations. True to the expectations, Indian Armed Forces have all along acquitted themselves with honour and grace being totally secular and professional. The inherent loyalty, dedication and readiness for sacrifice of our Forces make them darling of common citizens of the country. Surveys conducted by various agencies from time to time also corroborate this fact. The armed forces of India have large coastal and land border to defend; coupled with this is the internal strife which when beyond police forces, needs to be mostly addressed by armed forces of the country. Accordingly, the spread of our armed forces is through length and breadth of the country in form of numerous military, naval and air force stations. These stations are independently sustained administrative and security power centres, seen as instruments of progress and development in the areas of their influence. Military stations, garrisons and cantonments have a great role in keeping the nation secure, prosperous and integrated.

The locations of cantonments and garrisons in India are mostly a British legacy. The British had very thoughtfully cited each defence station and a close look reveals the rationale behind locating them. During the expansion of East India Company's operations in the country, there was requirement of inherent protection for their factories, ships, offices and residences; and later, imperial interests[1]. Before 1857, many hill areas were also developed for habitation of British officers as these gave them compatible climatic conditions of their country. Such areas also needed security and administrative support, and thus, garrisons and cantonments were also planned at these stations; though these were less of tactical and more of administrative in nature. After 1857, however, requirements were different and new military stations were created mostly in north India, with the aim of keeping the native forces dispersed.

India currently has 77 cantonments in 17 different states. Creation of any new cantonment, especially in remote areas is seen as a step towards improving economic and infrastructural status of that area. This is due to connected development in terms of creation of road network, business opportunities, better schooling facilities and improved health care in these areas. Indian states with army presence are marked on the map below.

---

[1] Cantt do spirit - Indian Express, Jul 21,2009.

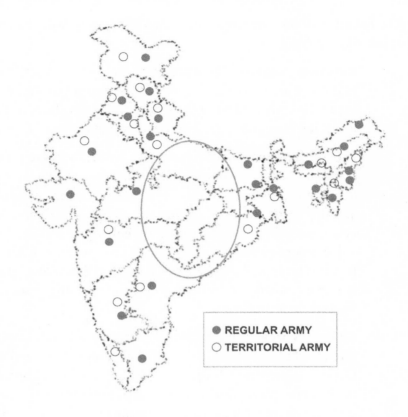

Map 2

Contribution of Cantonments and Garrisons in the Society

After India got independence in 1947, there were hardly any changes that were brought to the existing structure of the army and locations of cantonments and garrisons continued to be generally same. 'Hill Retreats' made as garrisons by the British are still functional. These are mostly being used now as training hubs by Indian armed forces. Other stations in plains are being used as peace stations for peace tenures of the units who have to move to hard field or counter insurgency areas on their turn. The dispersal of cantonments done by the British for other reasons has proved to be blessing in disguise for our country in two aspects; firstly, such a large army could not be located at limited stations; and secondly, their presence across the country has brought army closer to society. There is no denying the fact that military stations have contributed immensely in development of our society. Some of the important effects are:-

- **Inherent Security.** Presence of an armed forces station in a particular area ensures security to the people of the region. Other than physical security, these stations also lead to social, financial, psychological and environmental security.

- **Infrastructural Development.** Wherever there are military stations, improved communication network, electric and telephone connectivity can be seen in the areas around. In addition to these basic facilities, most stations in remote areas also have helipads that are used for helicopter service during any emergency both by defence and civil personnel. All such features bring in a change in the basic outlook of local people which eventually contributes in they identifying themselves as active part of the nation.

- **Economic Development.** Employment opportunities created through Station Head Quarters, MES, Station CSD and other Depots; contribute a lot in improving the financial health of the local people. Military stations also provide ready markets for local people. Consequently, opening up of small business outlets, expansion of cottage industry like dairy, poultry, vegetables, fruits and other local produce brings in financial freedom amongst common masses.

- **Environmental Development.** Military stations have a great share in arresting environmental degradation in the country. They are the role models in the field of preserving greenery and ecology. A special emphasis is given to landscaping, afforestation and plantation in military garrisons. Besides being a motivational factor to locals, this initiative provides them with clean and green environment.

- **Social Impact.** Defence stations contribute in social development of the country in a big way. Creation of hospitals, schools and other welfare related projects has a positive bearing on the social development of the local people. Families and children of ex-servicemen of the area are highly benefitted from service hospitals and schools. Army/Navy/Air Force schools in the country have equally benefitted civilian families also. Military stations also contribute constructively in maintaining social balance by arresting exodus of people that takes place towards bigger cities in search of jobs and employment.

- **Motivational Effect.** Numerous intangible benefits are inadvertently passed on to the society by virtue of defence stations being in the vicinity. These have long lasting effects on peoples' minds. People see a system in place amidst them which functions despite all odds. They see disciplined layouts and methodical ways of doing things; and this has a positive lesson for the people.

Raising of TA Units in Parts of Country Devoid of Armed Forces Signature

It has been amply clarified that presence of armed forces' station in an area is one of the main factors responsible for bringing in progress and prosperity to that area. It is an historical fact that in olden times also all garrisons had developed townships around them. Such townships became trading centres for local population and were key to social and economic upliftment of the society. Development of cities like Kolkata, Delhi, Agra, Shimla, Surat, Pune, MHOW, BABINA, Jhansi and townships grown around ASSAM RIFLES units in the NE, can be attributed to presence of strong army bases there at different times. In fact, the civilization has always been linked to the security establishment and both have been complementary to each other.

There are still some crucial parts of the country where footprint of armed forces is missing (Map 2 refers). These are mostly remote and tribal areas devoid of basic development. These are the very areas where due to lack of infrastructure and social development, local habitants have turned rebellious and started challenging the national writ. These people may be right in a way because the hand of governance, per say, has not reached these areas even after 65 years of independence. These people are being exploited by big companies and their produce is purchased by them for negligible monetary returns. Their age old habitats are being threatened to be acquired for commercial activities causing problems for their survival. On analysis of Map 2 and Map 3, it is quite clear that naxals and other extremist elements are freely operating in areas where military stations and such defence establishments are sparsely/not located. It will be worthwhile effort to have a qualified body carrying out a detailed project study on social and economic impact of armed forces' presence in areas where they are permanently located vis-à-vis other areas devoid of their presence. A very clear and interesting picture will emerge.

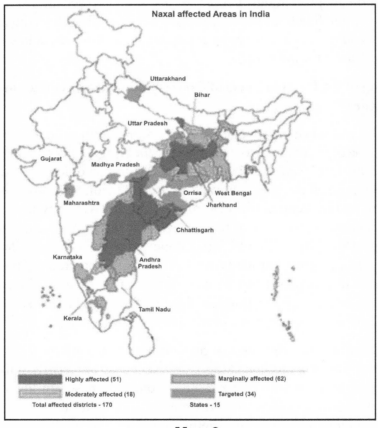

Map 3

Map 3 depicts areas affected by Naxalism in India. A serious and deliberate development plan, tailor-made for each affected area, needs to be evolved to bring locals at par with rest of the countrymen. A balanced long term plan, in consonance with the aspirations of local people is required; which besides providing them with their legitimate dues also honours their life style, customs and traditions. To start with, armed forces must have their locational presence in these areas. The most suited army units that can be thought about for these areas will be TA units. Within TA also, the best bet could be H&H TA units. The uniqueness of H&H TA units is their ability to recruit people on local region/district levels. This feature will ensure that local unemployed youth of a particular area gets a fair chance and is absorbed in the security mechanism. Raising of H&H TA units can be a part of the development package that is planned for these areas. Local youth who till now is potential raw material for future anti-national movements, can be brought into mainstream by giving opportunity of recruitment in H&H TA units. The personnel of these units, in addition to providing social and financial security to the people around, will also be handy against combating natural calamities and other man-made disasters. The concept of H&H has worked very well both, in J&K and North-Eastern states. However, one thing is required to be considered before taking this step. Army/H&H TA units cannot be raised in isolation to function in areas deprived of matching administrative support. There is, thus, a requirement of creating military infrastructure in terms of sidestepping some formation, training centre, depot, defence PSU alongside a station headquarter in each planned target area. H&H TA units raised in the area can then function smoothly around such an administrative centre. Also, the infrastructure required for other civic development can be built around these military stations by the respective state governments; creation of which till now has been a big challenge. There may be initial setbacks in trying this experiment, but long term results would be in broader national interest. With more and more people joining mainstream, strength of anti-national elements will ultimately diminish. This whole cycle for a particular area may take 15-20 years of time.

The Way Ahead

It must be appreciated by the countrymen that 'we shall exist if only the state exists'. Towards this realization, it is extremely important to decide and act fast to bring hitherto left out areas under the influence-umbrella of armed forces of the country. The decision to create more cantonments/military stations should be holistic; based on past experiences and should consider not only disturbed areas but left out peaceful areas as well. This, besides providing equal opportunities to all citizens, will also ensure future cohesion of the country. It is not that these issues have not been debated in the past but the hurdle is; fast decision making and execution. It had been conveyed to the nation that very soon TA units consisting of local tribal would be raised[2] to bring in a sense of security in naxal hit areas of the country. The following issues need to be considered and followed under the directions of government:-

- 'In Principal' consensus within concerned Ministries on time bound comprehensive development plan for neglected areas.

- Identification of areas for development of cantonments and concurrent feasibility study on their sustenance.

- Inclusion of local representatives from the area while formulating road-map for the region.

- Concurrent raising of new cantonments and TA units.

- Infrastructure development under the security cover of state police and temporarily inducted/newly raised TA/army units, as is being done for creation of rail corridor in North Eastern states.

- Permanent resolution of problems like land holdings and jungle rights to local people, based on existing practices.

- Reaching out to separatist organisations for simultaneous dialogue for political solution.

The problem of left wing terrorism is quite old and has now taken deep roots in India. It is further penetrating into the society with each passing day. It has been openly admitted by no less than the Prime Minister of the country, Dr Manmohan Singh that naxalism/ left wing terrorism is the biggest internal threat to the country. As the problem is big, bigger remedial measures are required to be taken in acceptable time frame.

---

[2] An article in TOI dated 02 Mar 2012, 'Soon, tribal army to fight Reds', by Josy Joseph.

CHAPTER VIII

BALANCING REGULAR ARMY AND TERRITORIAL ARMY IN FUTURISTIC SCENARIO: A WAY FORWARD

"The soldier is the Army. No army is better than its soldiers. The soldier is also a citizen. In fact, the highest obligation and privilege of citizenship is that of bearing arms for one's country."

- George S Patton Jr

Ethos of Security

The concept of security in Indian context has multiple facets. More and more number of security agencies in the country, somehow, indicates the non-holistic approach in this regard. While chairing and speaking at one of the discussions at USI in August 2012, Lt Gen (Retd) VK Nayar, PVSM, SM, ex-Governor, Manipur, expressed his concern on the raising of so many different forces and connected headquarters in the country. "Number of different forces cannot resolve the situation and additional headquarters will not add to the bite", he said. The thought by the General has a great message. Each force that comes into being has to live up to prove its existence by way of results. In this process, at times, a sense of one-upmanship is generated and highjacks the actual agenda of the force for which it was raised. Limited gains achieved within own domain, are overly exaggerated with the aim of taking quick credit which leads to unwarranted turf wars amongst different agencies. In India, the creation of a new set up is generally hailed with fanfare and taken as a step towards advancement and progress. But, basic parameters needed for successful running of the organization; like accountability, administration, sustenance, quantum of inter-dependence by sharing of efforts/resources with sister agencies and periodic evaluation, are disregarded. The creation of a new public body is taken as destined to last till posterity. This modus-operandi of working needs to be changed. Any organization or body that is created should have definite objective and on its accomplishment, should either cease to exist or reorganized/ redeployed on need basis. If this practice is not started in near future, the bulk of our budgetary resources will be used up for only administration and upkeep of our organisations. A very rational and pragmatic view, therefore, needs to be taken on creation of government bodies. Before creating any organisation, the objective is required to be clearly defined and terms of reference specified as regards time line and results. This rule should be applicable to all; including security forces of the country.

Talking of security forces, a broad road map catering for various extreme contingencies; in sync with national objectives, policies and international obligations, needs to be drawn out for next 30 to 40 years in advance. This will broadly spell out future requirement of forces in terms of strength, capability and budgetary support. Once guidelines are in place, it will be much easier to meet set objectives in a time-bound manner. Deviations encountered can always be addressed applying mid-course evaluations and corrections. Advance planning in security related subjects is mandatory as national requirements cannot wait. It must be appreciated that the strength of security forces cannot be enhanced in a short period as is possible in other departments. It takes years to nurture a recruit and transform him into a complete soldier; fit to take on varied security challenges. A fine balance, therefore, needs to be made regarding strength requirement of our armed forces in future. In this regard, there is always a dichotomy in the requirement of having minimum adequate strength vis-à-vis capability of enhancing it within acceptable time frame. This is where importance of part-time force (in our case TA) comes in. The country ought to have adequate trained part-time citizens available to be easily mobilized during national emergencies. This option will always offset the option of raising newer units at the time of requirement. This is up to the 'think-tank' at government level to perceive and decide how our country is going to dispose itself in future and what role will be there for the armed forces of the country in the overall game plan.

Strength Requirement of Army in Present Scenario

The present strength of army in India is approximately 11.55 lakhs including 35,000 of TA strength. In addition to this, MoD has raised DSC for the security of static military installations during peace time. This force caters for lateral induction of ex- servicemen of army and personnel from TA battalions. The approximate present strength of this force is 60,000 which is likely to be enhanced considerably by end of 12th plan. The army at present is committed for security of long land borders with China, Pakistan, Nepal, Bangladesh and Myanmar. Besides, it is overly embroiled in resolving internal security problems of the country.

China's economic development coupled with its massive infrastructure improvement drive along Indian borders in the North and East cannot be just overlooked. Though it is correct to assume that full-fledged war in future context between countries having nuclear weapons is not possible, but power projection by China against competitor India will continue in one way or the other in times to come. This also indicates that China does not wish to normalize relations by settling down border issues and will continue compelling India to commit more and more of its money on defence related infrastructure. Moral and material support to separatist organisations will give it much better returns than what full war can give.

On the Western side, India has a potential but politically unstable neighbour to guard against. It has its own compulsions to keep India engaged in fighting proxy war. Although, it is not a declared war, but war in this form has been on for a long time. Because of its fixation to keep India bleeding through thousand cuts, Pakistan, in the bargain has compromised on its own peace and progress. It has reached a stage of no return. It will not be a surprise to see total anarchy in Pakistan in next 20-30 years. Such a situation will again be dangerous to India.

The commitment of forces fighting against terrorism is not as much in neighbouring countries as in India. The price of having a multi-cultural and secular society is quite heavy in terms of both social and economic fields. The neighbour nations exploit this multi-cultural arrangement by injecting divisive sentiments based on religion and region amongst our uneducated masses. As India is surrounded by big and small neighbours, our approach at this critical juncture should be to take along maximum of our smaller neighbours as equal partners. They are sovereign nations and will stay with India only if they are treated with respect and their national interests are honoured. They have to be dealt with utmost care and their aspirations should be regarded. This will ensure that relations remain healthy and borders with them do not have to be overly guarded the way it is done with China and Pakistan. The old philosophy that a weak person would not become rogue and harm you unless he is totally humiliated and cornered, holds good for our relations with smaller neighbours as well.

Considering the problems and requirement of troops for countering hostile Pakistan on its West, aggressive China on the North and other smaller neighbours playing presently on a delicate turf, India is treading a very tight rope. The idea of reducing its regular armed forces in such a scenario may not hold ground. Political efforts, however, should continue to create an environment where all neighbours start concentrating on their economies and social developments. Trust deficit can be politically bridged by engaging them in dialogue and instituting enhanced confidence building measures. Money expended on such efforts would be far less than what would otherwise be spent on expanding infrastructure and military hardware. Later, in some future scenario when border dispute with China is resolved, Pakistan starts seeing some logic in improved relations with India by shunning its support to terrorist organizations, other neighbours start prospering making use of Indian markets and internal security situation within the country stabilises, the strength of regular armed forces may be justified to be reduced by couple of lakhs. But the fact remains that if today, India has to face three pronged threat; from China, Pakistan and internal elements, it needs some preparation in advance by way of trained reserves that could be built upon and mobilized to fill the vacuum. As a prelude to that situation, the reserve part-time component must be strengthened so as to have capability readily available for any sudden build up. For this transformation to be workable and seamless, efforts have to start now.

Selective TA-isation of Army

The enabling of our reserves to be capable of replacing the regular component of army; presently engaged in counter insurgency operations, during conventional war, will be a long drawn process. The primary requisite to enhance capability of part-time force is to standardize its equipment holding. This has to be made at par with regular infantry battalion. By instituting this singular factor, utility and performance of this force can enhance manifold. The balancing of regular and part-time components in army has to be holistically seen without any prejudice. There are some ways by which a start can be made:-

- **TA-isation of an Infantry Battalion.** In Japanese Army, each unit of regular army has a part-time subunit in it [1]. This can be replicated in our defensive formations by trying out various models suiting to our requirements. Three models are suggested to be tried for their efficacy before implementation:-

    o **Model I.** Battalion Headquarters to remain on regular basis. Out of four Rifle Companies, two to remain on regular basis and two to be brought on Headquarters basis i.e. TA-ised. In Mortar Platoon, two sections to remain on regular basis and one section to be TA-ised. 50 percent strength of Anti-Tank Guided Missile, Signal and Administration elements to be regular and balance to be TA-ised. If eventually even if 300 personnel are brought on TA concept in a battalion, the saving in terms of money would be roughly 11 crore for each battalion every year. Calculated for 319 battalions [2], it works out to recurring amount of 3509 crore per annum as salary of serving personnel and additional 1148 crore every year as pension liability for retirees.

    o **Model II.** Battalion Headquarters to remain on regular

---

[1] Discussion with Lt Gen (Retd) PC Katoch, PVSM, UYSM, AVSM, SC, Council Member, USI.

[2] Understanding India's Military by Ali Ahmed, IDSA.

basis. Out of the four Rifle Companies, three Companies to remain on regular basis and one Company to be brought on Headquarters basis. Mortar Platoon should not be touched. 50 percent manpower in Anti-Tank Guided Missile, Signals and Administration elements to be regulars and balance to be TA-ised. The cost savings (150 personnel) in this model @ 5.5 crore for each battalion per annum would be 1755 crore for 319 battalions in a year towards salary. An additional saving of 574 crore would be possible because of reduced pension liability.

o   **Model III**. Battalion Headquarters to remain on regular basis. Out of four Rifle Companies, one Company to remain regular and three to be brought on Headquarters basis (TA-ised). In Mortar Platoon, two sections each to be on regular and TA concept. In Anti-Tank Guided Missile, Signals and Administration elements, 50 percent strength in each to be kept on regular and TA basis. The saving to the exchequer @16.5 crore per battalion per year would be 5263 crore from salaries and 1722 crore from pensions.

The above given models are a broad guideline for peacetime employment and can be further debated and modified as per ground requirements. A different model may be applicable to different Commands.

*   **Integral TA Battalion with Newly Raised Divisions.** To start with, it will be worthwhile to consider a battalion each of TA as integral part of newly raised divisions in the army. The embodiment of these battalions can be so synchronized that they are always available to the Commanders for two months during operational rehearsals and/or other exercises. This arrangement will ensure that less number of regular battalions are raised and also address the fear of voids that may be there in some formations. If three TA battalions (one each) are tried for three divisions, the total recurring saving every year will be approximately 87 crore.

*   **TA Battalion with Holding Divisions.** The TA battalions raised as integral to newly raised divisions must undergo

rigorous conditioning and training in their new role before they are declared fit for defensive operations. On carrying out their performance evaluation, a decision can then be taken whether to enlarge their domain. If operationally found up to mark, a TA battalion each with all holding divisions of the army can be planned. A newly raised TA battalion for a particular division should in all probabilities be located within operational boundaries of that division; or else, a battalion from outside should be nominated for permanent affiliation with that division. The advantage in both cases would be a dedicated battalion that will accrue permanency and continuity in operations. Such battalions in divisions, over the period of time, will become operational assets with their commanders. To start with, these battalions can be tried as reserve battalions of reserve brigades of the divisions. By taking a TA battalion each with 29 holding divisions[3], the cost saving to the exchequer per year works out to 841 crore from salary and 249 crore from pension liability.

- **Armoured TA Regiments with Holding RAPIDS**. Holding RAPID divisions, on the same lines as holding infantry divisions, can have one of the armoured regiments as TA armoured regiment to be employed as part of reserve brigade. These regiments can initially be raised by making use of obsolete equipment and later when the state improves, could be given matching equipment existing in that formation. Intangible benefits and savings will be there by raising such TA units.

- **TA Battalion in Holding Brigades.** The ultimate balancing between regular army and TA will be considered to have taken place when each holding brigade in the army will have a TA battalion as its part. After operational evaluation of TA battalions in holding role in the divisions for 10-15 years, if it is found that they are performing up to required standards, then there will not be a problem of a TA unit being accepted by holding Brigade Commanders as a third battalion in their

---

[3] 'The Military Balance' by International Institute for Strategic Studies, 2013.

brigades. If harnessed, this arrangement will create ample reserves and a holding corps would spare a division size force (9xbattalions from 3xdivisions). This will be extremely important for HQ Commands during actual operations. The comments expressed by Gen Shankar Roy Choudhury during the interactive session of seminar held at CLAWS, New Delhi in Nov 2004 are reproduced below:-

.....That may mean right sizing of army. If this holding role of our formations does not go away vis-à-vis Pakistan, which is major commitment of our army, are you prepared to have at least 50 percent of manpower in the holding formation from the TA? Are you prepared to take that step? Yes, we will have holding formations, in every brigade we will have two battalions of TA and one regular battalion. I have tried it a couple of times. My army commanders were up in arms. So you have to take these decisions, otherwise the army will not change.

......manpower is important; the thing is how to do it cheaply and not at the cost of the defence budget. Therefore, what is the future structure of the infantry, the largest component of Indian Army, and the land forces component of the integrated defence forces? Are you prepared to consider the infantry to be composed in various percentages of the TA, special forces and mechanized infantry? I mean, we must start thinking on these lines. Otherwise, nothing will change [4].

The annual cost savings to the exchequer with this model will be 2523 crore from salaries and 748 crore from pensions.

- **TA Battalions as Demonstration Battalions at Training Academies, Training Centres and Schools of Instruction.** Each training academy, centre and school requires a demonstration battalion for its training to be effective. Instead of dedicating a regular battalion for this activity, it will be administratively much easier and better to have a TA demonstration battalion in each training institution. The regular battalions can thus be relieved to hone their operational skills. As per the requirement and curriculum of

---

[4] Army 2020 – Shape, Size, Structure and General Doctrine for Emerging Challenges, edited by Lt Gen (Retd) Vijay Oberoi, PVSM, AVSM, VSM, Director, Centre for Land Warfare Studies.

trainees, companies of these battalions can be embodied and disembodied from time to time. Savings will be enormous even if these battalions are mandated to be embodied for six months.

- **Conversion of One Company in each RR Battalion into TA Company.** The Rashtriya Rifle(R&R) battalions were primarily raised for counter insurgency areas of J&K and North- Eastern states. These battalions generally have their fixed locations with manpower being periodically recycled. These units heavily rely on local support for intelligence and other administrative requirements. A company in each RR unit based on H&H concept of TA can be very useful for acquiring actionable intelligence and feeling the pulse of the people[5] .

The apprehensions of how TA units would perform in defensive role will be offset by the fact that since 2001, as against earlier one month recruit training at unit level, the TA recruit of today is being trained for nine months like his counterparts in regular army. During his training at Regimental Centre, he learns about all weapons, ammunitions and basic military tactics. The only two requirements of TA units that need to be kept in mind before switching over to the new model are:-

- Change in Role and Task of TA.

- Authorisation of weapons and ammunition at par with regular battalion.

The present role/task and equipment holding can continue to remain unchanged for Urban TA units whose troops follow weekend concept of training and may not be able to meet operational standards in holding formations. Urban TA units can continue to be deployed on existing tasks of guarding VAs/VPs and Rear Area Security (RAS) duties as hitherto fore.

To have an overview on what, the esteemed Committee ordered by H E General Sir Claude J E Auchinleck, the Commander in Chief of India, had to say in its report on role and equipment of TA[6] , it is

---

[5] Discussion with Lt Gen (Retd) H S Lidder, PVSM, UYSM, YSM, VSM.

[6] Reorganisation of the Army and Air Force in India, Report of a Committee set up by HE the Commander in Chief of India (Vol I) Oct – 1945.

reproduced below:-

> **General principles**. Before proceeding to discuss the forms in which a Territorial Army has hitherto existed in India and our own recommendations for its future organization, we would draw attention to certain principles which we consider should govern any force of this kind. The first of these is that the force should be essentially an integral part of the field army in war for combatant duties. If this condition is not fulfilled, high morale, which is no less important and much more difficult of attainment in territorial units than in regular units, will inevitably be lacking, and the recruits attracted will be of wrong type. The recruit whom we wish to attract and whom alone it is worthwhile enlisting and training is the citizen who desires, despite his civilian occupation, to fit himself to bear arms with distinction in a national emergency.

> **Characteristics of Territorial Army**. From this first principle follow others. The types of territorial units should be mainly non-technical. The place for a man who wishes and is required to perform in war military duties allied to his civil occupation is in the supplementary reserve. Territorial units must be closely associated with the corresponding regular units, and homogeneous with them in equipment, organization and as far as possible efficiency, since the two are to be inter-changeable in war. Territorial units must also be capable of replacing war wastage at the same rate as regular units, whether by using the regular army replacement system or by having some organization of their own for the purpose. Finally, efficiency in war is the sole justification of a territorial army, and none of the incidental benefits which it can confer, such as to stimulate and crystallize patriotic feeling, will accrue unless this condition is insisted upon. To maintain territorial units not likely to be an efficient part of the regular army in war is not only wasteful but does positive harm by bringing a potentially valuable institution into discredit.

The report was finalized in Oct 1945 for the benefit of free India. The Committee had visualized the problems that the TA was going to face about its role and other unequal grounds.

Attracting Talent for TA Units

If concept of TA is to be taken to a higher level and TA units are to be promoted to undertake defensive operations as part of holding Divisions/Brigades, then the strength of TA officers has to be made up well in time. As of now, in the absence of an officer, a JCO can command a TA company; but this will not hold well in the changed scenario. At present, the officer state in TA is much worse than what is there in regular army. Approximately 40 percent is the deficiency in officers' cadre. To fill this void, a national campaign is required to be launched to reach out to all departments, colleges, universities and corporate houses. The support from central government is also needed in this regard. An incentive based directive needs to be issued to government and non-government departments to spare their employees for commissioning into TA as part-timers. The unique concept of TA has to be made understood in right perspective to the target beneficiaries. Following are few of the measures that could be instituted to draw maximum participation from various departments:-

- Extensive advertisement campaign through print and electronic media.

- Regular interaction with colleges and universities through qualified teams.

- Motivation of NCC cadets to join TA in addition to their civil careers.

- Introduction of simplified application form and facility to applicants for filling of forms during interactions only.

- Online facility for forwarding applications and appearing for preliminary interviews.

- Yearly feedback to the government on number of employees enrolled from a particular department for timely release of incentives (if decided).

Numerous innovations can be devised to propagate the concept of TA amongst the masses. There are many people who do not want army as a full career but wish to be part of armed forces and give their services for limited periods. The problem is of tapping them and providing them an opportunity.

CHAPTER IX

SCOPE OF TA-ISATION IN VARIOUS ARMS AND SERVICE

"The problem in defense is how far you can go without destroying from within what you are trying to defend from without."

- Dwight D Eisenhower

In all fields of management, economy of effort is the buzzword. But, this is also true that whenever there is a talk about, 'Giving More by Using Less' in any organization, the perception created is, 'slashing of manpower'. This perception may be right in a way and can be broadly interpreted in two ways:-

(a) Capability/capacity can be enhanced using existing human resource by making use of newer technological advancements to achieve higher outputs.

(b) Man power can be slashed yet capability/capacity maintained by introducing new techniques and technology.

Both the above mentioned options are suited and can be used as per output requirements of any organization. In case of Army, like any other organization, there is a dual requirement and hence, both of the interpretations can be applied. There is a 'Fighting Component' (Combat Arms) in army, which requires fit, fully trained, sharp and cohesive units/subunits having well defined task for each of its members in the event of war. The second component in army is the 'Supporting Component' (Combat Support Arms). This component contains units that are responsible for providing close support to fighting arm units in terms of communication, artillery fire, aviation and air defence (AD). The third component of 'Logistic Support'

(Logistics Services), is equally important for the fighting component to enable execute its operations smoothly. It is this service component where introduction of new technology footprint to enhance quality output can be more agreeable in future. Starting from procurement/ production, storing, distribution and carriage to frontline fighting units, it can be better managed making use of new technology and management techniques – so far the domain of only corporates and big companies having global supply chains. Army can study the economic methods such companies are using. To have better efficiency in our inventory management and supply in the army, the logistic pipeline must be shrunk, load lightened and the closing time cut. An efficient and smooth logistic system can change the way army fights. The whole system has to be strategically responsive and dominant at each sphere of war. Beside introducing the technology in our logistic system, the transformation in doctrine, training, leadership, organisations, availability of material, matching installations and quality soldiers need to be concurrently brought in[1]. The introduction of technology should include and focus on exploiting improvements in automation, communication, business practices, refurbishing command and control relationships to provide better cohesion in the command and reduced logistic footprint. In short, each advancement or change at strategic level has to be deliberated upon in its entirety and matching logistic parameters need to be dovetailed in the beginning itself. The outsourcing of logistic support to the army can be considered and planned with big national companies engaged in supply activities. These companies can nominate their volunteer employees dealing with army stores to enroll themselves as part-time soldiers for their continuity during eventuality of war. They continue to be employees of a particular company and can be exercised in their desired role during army exercises by embodying them. Analysis of arms/services can be made whether part of their manpower can be TA-ised or made part timer.

Combat Arms

Combat arms - armoured corps, infantry and engineers which operate at the frontline during operations are organized and function

---

[1] USAWC Strategy Research Project, 'Transformation – Revolution in Military Logistics' by Lt Col Aundre F Piggee, US Army.

in a slightly different way than their support arms and logistics services comrades. Alongside their training and mastery over combat skills, greater emphasis is laid on inculcating team spirit, healthy competition, and camaraderie coupled with inter dependence. All these traits shine out and are strengthened when troops of such units live, train, exercise and operate together as unit/subunit teams. To bring in a sense of regimentation, troops are generally assigned only one unit where they serve till they retire. The unit of an individual in fighting arms is only changed if he is posted to a new raised unit or becomes a discipline case in his original unit.

It has been proved beyond doubt that a soldier fights and sacrifices for the honour of his unit, colours and identity. The country and cause are automatically looked after. A sense of belongingness to a particular outfit and being an important member of that family drives the individual to protect his Regiment's interests both in war and peace. In present organization of fighting units, even the tradesmen are combatants. They train and exercise along with brother combatants of the unit and are fully prepared to fight alongside them. All leaders and led in the unit work towards the same cause - *Izzat* of the unit. The loyalty and love towards his unit is so deeply engrained in the mind of a soldier that not only during his active service, but after retirement also, he is ready to fight as part of his unit, if given a chance.

In this backdrop, thinking about bringing a part time element into fighting units will be resented to. However, it is also a fact that today's soldier is more open in his approach and is more in touch with outside world than before. This approach has brought in better adaptability and more flexibility in him. Today's soldier sees things from different perspective and is more pragmatic in accepting organisational and functional changes. This aspect of soldier's changed perspective should not be taken as his vulnerability by the decision- makers while introducing modifications in the organisation; any change has to be necessity driven and in the overall interest of the army and the nation.

To bring in out sourcing or part-timeness in the fighting component of the army, specific trades have to be identified and a long term time matrix covering over 30 years duration needs to be drawn for implementation. This implementation cannot be thought about in isolation. Structural changes are required to be made in our peace time administration and war time requirements. Cantonments and other military peace stations need to be refurbished with state of art technology driven cook houses and messes. Repairs of vehicles and other instruments in peace stations need to be centralized and machinery robotized. The issue of over dependence of units on clerical staff in the absence of centralized network and inability of officers to exploit computers to their optimum potential, needs to be addressed. Centralised shops like laundry, hair saloon, and furniture and weapon repair facilities can be planned to be part of any future military station/ cantonment. With such centrally available facilities in military stations, the trades and manpower in a fighting unit that could be planned to be TA-ised or brought under part-time concept could be:-

- Staff involved in unit cook houses/messes.

- Tradesmen like barber, carpenter, blacksmith, washer man etc.

- Nominated clerical staff including SKT clerks.

- Some decided percentage of B vehicle drivers not belonging to fighting echelon of the unit.

To address the above mentioned suggested reshuffle, both peace and war time requirements need to be considered. Centrally run administrative shops will be run by people who are on part-time rolls of station units. These people will function on TA concept while in peace and will be embodied for limited periods to be part of the central mechanism as also for duties with their units during exercises and operational rehearsals. To meet the functional requirement, they can be embodied for complete duration of their units' tenure in field areas. The concept may look complex in the beginning but if tried and experimented with determination will certainly give dividends. Some of the suggested changes are already being practiced in the US army and working efficiently. In consonance with the changing times, technological and management driven reconstruction should start in our army at the earliest. Limited manpower that can be thought to be TA-ised in fighting arms is discussed below.

Armoured Corps. Scope of bringing in a part-time element in armoured regiments can be restricted to only selected tradesmen, clerks and B vehicle drivers. This strength can be TA-ised and maintained as central pool within the garrison/military station during peace tenures.

Infantry. In addition to above mentioned trades in armoured regiments, one out of four companies can be experimented to be TA-ised. This company will work on TA concept during the peace tenure of its unit (two month embodiment during operational rehearsal) and is fully embodied to accompany the unit for its field tenure. Exception of embodying TA-ised company while in peace location can be made when the unit is part of a strike formation. The issue has already been covered in detail in Chapter VIII.

Engineers. Engineers units are specialist in nature. Being specialist, limited manpower in terms of tradesmen, clerks and drivers can be TA-ised in them. However, personnel engaged in water supply, parameter fencing and pipe layout can be considered for TA-sation. This strength will generally work out to one platoon per Engineer regiment.

Combat Support Arms

This component of army is crucial for the smooth success of any military mission. Bombardments on enemy positions, before own attack by artillery is a pre requisite for a determined success. Air defence cover against hostile enemy air crafts coming to strike own concentrations of troops, equipment, command & control centers and other important infrastructure has tremendous value both at physical and psychological levels. Signals are another supporting arm which is the back bone of secure communication during war. The outcome of any operation solely depends on its efficient network in the combat zone. Another very important constituent of combat support arms is Aviation Corps. It acts as a force multiplier in its own way. Movement of commanders to points of decision, evacuation of causalities and ferrying of emergent supplies are some of the many tasks entrusted to Aviation.

Unlike in a combat arms unit, a soldier belonging to a unit of combat support arms is not stuck to one unit; he is posted to different units during his career. This makes him more adaptable and gives him more flexibility to function in changed circumstances. Although the success of any supporting arm unit also lies in the team work yet individual proficiency has more space in these units. The organization of these units can be made more compact by reducing over usage of combatants engaged in unit related administrative jobs. Economy in effort can also be brought in by ensuring outsourcing of all labour intensive tasks; handling of critical war related stores should only be done by combatants. This way, manpower can be saved, contributed towards station institutions and can be rotated as a part-time force working on TA concept.

Artillery. This support arm has three type of units under its fold; namely, Medium Artillery, Field Artillery and Light Artillery regiments. The manpower in an artillery unit is considerably less compared to an infantry battalion. However, considering the quantum of equipment held and role assigned to artillery units, there is scope to put some manpower on part-time concept during their peace tenures. As discussed for units of combat arms, artillery regiments can also spare their tradesmen (mess staff, barbers, carpenters, washer men etc), nominated clerks and light vehicle drivers to be pooled in the station pool which could operate on TA concept. In addition to this manpower, a battery in each artillery regiment can be considered for TA-isation. Such batteries can be embodied on annual basis for Field Firings and Practice Camps and fully embodied during regiments' field tenures. Equipment pertaining to these batteries can be preserved by mothballing on disembodiment of manpower.

Artillery Air Defence (AAD). Air defence units came into being in the Indian Army through TA route. Initially, two units of anti-aircraft force were raised before independence in early 40s which grew into a five unit force at independence during Indo-Pak conflict of 1947-48. The strength of these units rose to eight during Chinese aggression in 1962 and in 1971 there were 12 TA Air Defence units. Subsequently, in 1975, to maintain the crews at optimum efficiency, all TA Air Defence units were converted to regular Air Defence units.[2]

---

[2] The 'Citizens' Army', the Coffee Table Book of Additional Directorate General, Territorial Army.

Air Defence Artillery was part of Artillery till 1994 and thereafter it branched out as separate entity. In present context, 50 percent of the Artillery Air Defence units can be TA-ised. Only those national assets which require round the clock vigil should have dedicated air defence cover making use of regular units and balance 50 percent units should come back to TA concept with minimum permanent staff along with skeleton Regiment Headquarters for looking after the equipment and unit assets.

Signals. This is a very important technical arm that supports the army and has its footprint in all formations irrespective of nature of terrain and employment. It can be called as a 'software component' of army machinery. As discussed earlier in Chapter II, the automation of signal equipment and availability of satellites for improving secured communication in army has contributed in a big way in relieving pressure and work-load on soldiers. With these developments in place, there is a scope in a signal unit to identify and spare some manpower which can function on TA concept. Erstwhile large line laying parties and additional manpower committed on signal exchanges can be now considered to be TA-ised. A part of the saved manpower can be utilized for newly raised formations in field areas and other part can function on the concept of TA.

Aviation. The air component in army came into existence in 1986. Before its inception, the Air Force used to assist army in carrying out reconnaissance, causality evacuation and ferrying of Commanders in combat zone. It is a comparatively newer component and requires more time to stablise. Also, it being highly technical with impromptu tactical requirements, any core man-power working on part-time concept is not suggested. The only exception can be amalgamation of tradesmen and mess staff into station pool as part-timers.

Logistic Services

Logistics support is the back bone of any military campaign. However sophisticated and trained may be the fighting force, the most important aspect still remains the replenishment of arms, ammunition, combat stores and food supplies at right place and right time during the war. This is the pre requisite for success in the battle field. All successful campaigners in the past have laid maximum stress on this singular factor. In fact, in the modern warfare where time is at greater premium, greater planning is required to be done to organise uninterrupted logistics reach to all concerned in the combat zone. The world military history reveals that most military campaign failures could be attributed to incoherence between operational plans and the logistics support capabilities. As is suggested earlier in the chapter, more scientific techniques of provisioning, transporting and distributing the logistics supplies have to be introduced in Services. Much has been said on having a Logistics Command for our armed forces to coordinate logistics supplies across the board but nothing concrete seems to have evolved so far. The creation of Logistics Command will give tangible results in fields of efficiency and prioritisation of logistics supplies as also to bring in economy in human effort. The British system has achieved a turnaround in last fifty years following a clear line of action[3]. They successfully introduced:-

- Computerized logistics management.

- Integration of all intra-service activities on conventional logistics.

- Corporatisation of repair infrastructure.

- Privatization of repair infrastructure followed by outsourcing of other support infrastructure.

- Integration of all inter-service logistics, under broad heads of Defence Logistics Organisation (DLO) and Defence Procurement Agency (DPA).

Introduction of similar measures in Indian army will reduce the unwarranted pressure on commanders and staff. In addition to bringing orderliness, transparency and uniformity in logistics chain; these measures will exponentially reduce the dependence on human resource. Manpower can be identified within various logistics corps which can thus be made as reserve that functions on part-time concept.

Ordnance Corps. The corps has an effective strength of approximately 55,000 personnel including about 20,000 civilian employees for peak

---

[3] 'Revolution in Military Logistics' by Rear Adm AP Revi; Issue Vol 23.3 Jul-Sep 2008 dt 14 Feb 2012.

time requirements. However, the peak requirement is only witnessed during a war; which means that manpower enrolled, though required to be there on rolls yet can be declared surplus and made part-time. This identified manpower can be kept abreast with its trade by calling up for two months engagement every year during normal times. Ordnance Corps has the potential of identifying at least 50 percent of civilian employees as part-timers. In fact, as of now, the work culture in branches of army having civilians has two distinct shades; one, of combatants having clear charter of work ordained under army orders and two, of civilians bound by lenient orders. In such scenarios, it becomes extremely difficult to work out the required balance in administering two wings which are following diverse work cultures. To avoid this dual administrative control in the corps as also in many other branches of army, it is suggested to get away with civil wings of employees and in turn enroll combatants based on the concept of TA as part-timers. This will bring in a much awaited discipline and service ethos into the functioning of the corps. To start with, employees identified to be made part-timers can be converted into TA and made to complete their engagement as per TA rules. All those civilians opposed to this arrangement may be given 'golden hand shake' and discharged.

Army Service Corps (ASC). ASC is primarily responsible for provisioning, procuring and distribution of supplies, transport, fuel oils and lubricants, hygiene chemicals and miscellaneous items to Army, Air Force and when required to Navy and other PMFs. In terms of manpower, the strength of ASC is approximately 77,000. Though the requirement of ASC supplies remains almost same round the year yet with introduction of modern techniques and selective out-sourcing of identified items, dependence on manpower can be reduced. Supplies up till Division HQ should be the responsibility of contracted agency. Third line transport battalions operating under HQ Commands/Areas/Sub Areas should be converted to TA transport battalions to be embodied as on required basis for winter stocking or bulk stocking in high altitude/field areas. In addition, they can be embodied during formation exercises to bring in realism and imparting training to drivers.

Electronic and Mechanical Engineers (EME). EME is a major constituent of Indian Army and constitutes approximately 10 percent of the total strength. Its main job is to keep army operationally ready by keeping its electric, mechanical, electronic and optical equipment in state of war fitness. For EME to operate in battle zone, it is affiliated with fighting units as Forward Repair Teams (FRT)/Light Repair Workshops (LRW) to provide situational repair and recovery effort to the defective equipment. The support in the rear comes from Field Workshops which undertake repairs that are beyond FRT/LRW. Repairs of still bigger nature are sent to Station Workshops and Base Workshops. These are the workshops where there is a mix of regular army personnel and civilian employees. Here the introduction of part-time soldiers can be thought about. Many studies on transformation of repair chain in Indian Army suggest that manpower in Base Workshops and below should be provided by the contracted company and that these workshops should be maintained at their cost. Native companies like TATA, Ashok Leyland, Mahindra, BEL, BHEL, Bajaj Electricals etc should not have any problems accepting such an offer if they are involved in supply of their equipment to the army. If that is realized, all civil employees of a particular company can be enrolled as TA personnel on the lines of departmental TA units. For ten months, they are paid for by the company they belong to and for balance two months they get embodied as soldiers of TA and paid for by MoD. During general mobilization, the complete manpower gets embodied and works as a cohesive TA unit under MoD. The savings in terms of manpower and money will be enormous.

Analysis. The creation of much talked about 'Logistics Corps' primarily aimed at reducing the 'Teeth to Tail' ratio for faster mobilization of supplies, has been pending. The same needs to be suitably modified and tried to suit ground realities.

Identification of manpower in various arms/services for TA-isation is in no means an endeavour to undermine existing homogeneity in command structure but is to only suggest ways and means to optimise capacity. The analysis will help enable the authorities to make use of bringing part-time concept into nominated trades and, if situation so demands, sidestep these vacancies to proposed regular units planned for future expansion. The country at present is in evolving stage where there is no leeway for either-or equation. The ground realities compel

India to have large standing army equipped with latest technology and well trained and motivated reserves in terms of volunteer participation by awakened citizens. The concept of citizens joining voluntarily into the defence of the country needs to be vigorously reintroduced and propagated within our entire civil stream. In the initial years after independence, the concept of TA was talked and discussed about. The involvement of government in propagating the TA concept has been highlighted below by way of an article published in 'The Hindu' dated 30 May, 1958[4].

TERRITORIAL FORCE

An appeal to industrialists to help to promote public interest in the territorial and other auxiliary forces which were playing a very useful part in maintaining national solidarity and in the defence of the country was made by Mr. V.K. Krishna Menon, Defence Minister, during a meeting at Rajaji hall, Madras, on May 28. The State Government convened this preliminary meeting with a view to forming an association in Madras similar to the Welfare Association for Auxiliary Forces formed in Bombay under the guidance of Mr. Naval H. Tata. The objects of the association were to promote public interest in territorial and other auxiliary forces, assist in recruitment to them, encourage liaison between the various forces and the services and provide amenities and comforts for the units and member of the services.

---

[4] Territorials.blogspot.com/ – Passion not Profession, Major Surender Singh.

CHAPTER X

NEW AREAS FOR TERRITORIAL ARMY

"I am concerned for the security of our great Nation; not so much because of any threat from without, but because of the insidious forces working from within."

- Douglas MacArthur

The concept of part-time participation by citizens in the defence of the nation, in addition to their primary professions, firmly exists in our country; though with a slightly low priority. As amplified earlier, the concept is powerful enough to cater for varied future requirements of army for national security. The meaning of 'national security' is changing world over and has become more inclusive. As modes of waging wars are not restricted to borders alone, the war fighting capabilities have to be accordingly changed. Integration of local citizens into the overall security scheme has to be deliberately planned and volunteer participation by citizens made more attractive by opening new areas. To enable the Nation to enhance its war potential, greater number of country's population needs to be enrolled into TA and given mandatory training in weapons and field craft. At the time of war, interested soldiers may even be asked to join regular units. This will give ready made and trained manpower to the army to make up the deficiencies and losses.

The main aim of propagating peoples' participation in defence of the country is to create reserves in various fields which could be affiliated to the different organs of the armed forces. Each arm/ service of all three services has to analyse its task at hand, resources available and war wastage rate. This will enable them to come up with a requirement of part-time force that could be in accretion to its authorized war establishment. Suitably trained part-time TA battalions can be raised for identified areas and arms/services. Similarly, in the society also, there is a scope to address many sectors where part-time force can be of great help. After the success of Ecological TA Battalions sponsored by Ministry of Environment and Forests (MoEF)/State governments, it is well established that an important issue such as environment can be addressed at two fronts – one with concerned central/state departments themselves and the other with Task Forces like Ecological TA Battalions raised on regional ex-servicemen. This can be replicated in many other sensitive areas of the society where existing efforts seem to be inadequate to arrest the losses. Such participatory efforts leading to raising of TA battalions, in addition to raising of social and environmental standards in time bound manner, also contribute in rehabilitation of retired young soldiers. Few new areas that can be thought to be tested by peoples' part-time participation are divided into four parts:-

- Society
- Army
- Navy
- Air force

Society

Generally, all services in social sector come under one or the other government department. For each service; systems, procedures, checks and balances are in place, but still due to exploding requirements or complacency in priority identification, certain key areas fall prey to neglect. It is felt that all important areas should have duplicate structures to achieve following three aims:-

- To cope up with increased requirement.

- To bring in competitiveness within the departments to improve performance and efficiency in delivery system.

- To create a reserve force in a particular discipline that can be used during war/war like situations by the army.

Some of the areas that seem to be critical and have the potential for more thrust are analysed in following paragraphs.

Power Sector. This is one sector where the resource is scarce and demand is more. There is always a seasonal periodic spurt of additional requirement and thus, there is a requirement of critically monitoring the transmission and distribution of power to the users. Central Ministry controls main power grids and within states; stepping up, transmission and distribution mechanisms are there in place to control consumption. At both Centre and State levels there are huge transmission losses and power thefts. It is worthwhile to raise TA battalions to address the issue.

Power sector TA battalions can be raised on the lines of Ecological TA battalions constituting ex-servicemen from EME, Engineers and Signals. These battalions, by virtue of their task, should be affiliated to Corps of EME. Embodiment periods of such battalions can be between 6-8 months every year as per peak requirements of the department. These can be sponsored by Centre/State governments as per their tasking and requirement. At the time of general mobilization for war, these units will be embodied and operate under Ministry of Defence (MoD) for preparatory tasks at various Station and Base Workshops as accretion force. Also, during war, this manpower will be readily available for enhanced security duties at various thermal, hydro and nuclear power plants. Such units will be a boon both for war and peace time deployments.

Another type of power sector TA units can be raised on the lines of departmental TA units existing in Oil Sector. These units will be based on the employees of the power sector (power plants and grids) who get voluntarily enrolled into TA. Such units are officered by a mix of army and concerned departmental officers and are embodied as and when required, by the MoD on the recommendations of concerned ministry. These units are specifically raised for the concerned department, basically to achieve two aims. Firstly, to bring in army ethos and culture in functioning of the plant; and secondly, to counter any sabotage by the employees engaged in power supply operations, by way of going on strikes and agitations.

The third type of Power Sector TA units can be raised in big cities by concerned State governments; either based on civil population, ex-servicemen or mix of both to check power thefts and over-loadings during peak seasons. Such units are funded by state governments and can be directly placed under the State ministry for immediate action on their field reports. These units can be embodied during required months after approval of MoD. For the duration they are mobilized for army tasks during war or emergency, these units will be funded by MoD.

Highways. With rapid infrastructural development taking place in the country and with opening up of economy, the living standards and purchasing power of the population is growing by the day. To save time and effort, more and more people prefer individual modes of conveyance. Increase in number of vehicles in public transport and in private domain has put tremendous pressure on existing highways. The sudden spurt in number of vehicles in last decade or so has led to gross mismatch in highway development and vehicular growth. This factor alone is the cause of traffic jams, lower speeds and delays in movements of goods. The problem can be addressed and movement time can be shrunk by managing existing infrastructure in more judicious manner. Here again, TA units are the answer. To start with, few important highways which witness greater volumes of military and civil traffic should be identified and handed over to specially raised TA units which are affiliated to the Corps of Military Police and have requisite training and expertise to deal with traffic related issues. Such units, in addition to their peace time employment of keeping highways and choke points free from congestions, will also be ready made trained asset for war time requirements when military is mobilized along with its men and material. They will also be trained in recovery of defective vehicles and casualties during any accidents. These units should be funded by Ministry of Roads and Surface Transport for their peace time employment and by MoD for operational embodiments during war. The enrolment in these units can be from civil volunteers of a particular region; akin to Infantry

TA units. They need to have close liaison with respective state and traffic police forces. Bulk of the manpower of these units can be embodied during the seasons when maximum military units/convoys move towards their training areas, field firings, practice camps and winter stocking destinations. Highway TA units can be requested to be raised both by Ministry of Road and Surface Transport at the centre for national highways, and by State governments for state highways, as per their requirements.

Disaster Relief. Disaster management is another key area where peoples' participation by way of TA units can be exploited for social good. Each state government should plan to raise such units based on local volunteers to cater for natural calamities within states. These units can be affiliated to Corps of Engineers of the army and will be trained to handle disaster related tasks. For their specialized task, they will be equipped accordingly. The locations of these units can be decided by the state administration based on their past experiences and units' ability to be effective in acceptable time frame. The details of raising H&H TA units for such a task have been adequately covered in Chapter VI.

In addition to State sponsored dual task H&H TA units specifically meant for states, MHA sponsored dual task TA units raised on the lines of Infantry Battalion TA would be ideally suited to address disaster related issues at the national level. Such units; in addition to dealing with local emergencies, will also be liable to be employed in other parts of the country. These will be more useful in areas where disaster related incidents take place periodically and for prolonged periods of time. Besides, these units can also be used to provide aid to civil administration during critical times. Such units can be raised under MoD, to be funded by MHA. Their embodiment for army related tasks during war would be funded by MoD.

Tiger Reserves. In recent years there has been a great loss of tigers in national tiger reserves across the country by way of poaching and poor management. The tiger numbers have plummeted to dangerously low levels. Alarmed by this declining trend, the Prime Minister had to get involved himself and take initiative to bring the issue of 'Project Tiger' directly under his own supervision. The seriousness shown by the PMO sent a strong message to people presently involved in the security and administration of various Tiger Projects. However, no worthwhile change has been noticed in the recent past; poachers are becoming bolder by the day and operating as organized mafia. The success of poachers can be attributed to the un-coordinated security mechanism and collusion of poachers with greedy people employed on security duties. It has been proved beyond doubt that existing security apparatus tasked to provide protection to Tiger Reserves has become defunct. The main reason of failure is non-accountability at all levels. Some very effective measures by bringing in major structural changes in security mechanism of Tiger Projects have to be introduced to re-energise the whole apparatus. It is a common wisdom that the protection of any natural resource cannot be accomplished without the willing participation of natives of the area. To that end, efforts are needed to involve local population and sensitise them towards importance of conservation of flora and fauna. Locals will only cooperate in conservation affairs once they start getting sustainable income in return for their contribution. Involvement of people through TA task forces can be the answer. These units can be raised by enrolling local people and ex-servicemen of the concerned states/regions to address the menace of poaching and smuggling of tiger skins and their other body parts. With Tiger Reserve TA units in place, following related problems can also be resolved:-

- Protection of forest medical teams involved in providing medical care to tigers.

- Protection of census parties.

- Regulation of civilian tourists.

- Check on timber smuggling and illegal mining activities.

- Conservation of flora and fauna.

The terms and conditions for raising TA units, exclusively for Tiger Projects can be on the lines of Ecological TA units which are already successful. As regards funding, they will operate under MoEF; as is being done for Ecological units. If tried with will and passion, the involvement of army in conservation of tigers can be a useful experiment like ecological battalions.

River Restoration. Army is an epitome of security and good order in the society. It is called upon to control the situation and restore confidence amongst the masses when all other designed means tend to fail. It has constructively contributed in arresting degrading internal security as well as environmental security in the country; over and above its actual role of defending nation's sovereignty from outward interferences. A very important and controversial field in our society; which possibly qualifies to be given to the Armed Forces, is restoration operations of our major rivers in the country. Despite central and state governments having spent huge amounts of money, time and energy on this singular problem, nothing worthwhile has been achieved in return. The deteriorating condition of rivers of national importance is a cause of grave concern for the environmentalists of the country as lot many unforeseen problems are attached to this neglect. Nearly 80 percent of sewage generated in our country flows untreated into its rivers, lakes and ponds, turning the water sources too polluted to use. This figure was revealed at a meeting of experts on sewage and water issues organized by the Centre for Science and Environment as part of the 'Anil Agarwal Dialogues' series. Speaking at the conference, the Vice President Hamid Ansari said, "Indian cities produce nearly 40,000 million litres of sewage per day, enough to irrigate nine million hectares and barely 20 percent of this is treated."[1] Coming to specifics, degrading condition of the Yamuna river is no secret. Due to tonnes of industrial waste being released into this river at Yamuna Nagar, Panipat and Sonepat, presence of heavy metals have been seen in water that is picked up at Wazirabad reservoir to meet Delhi's drinking water needs[2]. The quality of water in other major rivers is also below standards. The administration has not been able to read the situation judiciously and instead of showing concrete plans on ground, had always been busy playing blame games. After carrying out futile exercises protracted over many years and a lot of money having gone down the drain, it is presumed that involvement of Army in this field can pay rich dividends. The only component within the army that can successfully undertake such a task is TA component. River Restoration

[1] *Times of India* newspaper report dated 05 Mar 2013.

[2] *Times of India* newspaper report dated 11 Mar 2013.

Force consisting of TA battalions raised on the lines of Ecological TA battalions is the answer to combat factors responsible for degradation and pollution of rivers in the country. Such an initiative at national level is extremely urgent as quality of water for drinking, irrigation purposes and aquatic life is turning to be highly dangerous in our rivers. The uncoordinated urbanization and industrialisation with no clear cut liability for its waste disposal on owners coupled with poor monitoring from government side is one of the primary reasons for the present mess. The exponentially expanding population has to be sensitised for their responsibility towards keeping our river-wealth in clean and healthy state to contribute positively in our day to day lives.

Proposed TA battalions can work in collaboration with government departments that are engaged in sewage-water treatment, control of industrial pollutants, recycling of organic/non-organic waste and highway/housing construction agencies working in close vicinities of threatened rivers. These TA units can be Engineers based units with required equipment authorised to them as per their assigned task. They can be located along identified river lines to execute and oversee their restoration work. The funding of the units can be pooled in by central and respective state governments as per the lay of the river. For better results, the enrolment in each unit should be based on the pattern being followed in H&H and Ecological battalions - a healthy mix of locals and ex-servicemen. Their tasking and operational domain has to be deliberately spelt out to have smooth cooperation with civil departments. A mechanism needs to be created to ensure cooperation from locals and various other NGOs already engaged in river restoration work. A time bound and focused approach will certainly reverse the existing poor state of our rivers. To start with, one river can be identified for its restoration and TA units for the same should be raised in collaboration with TA Directorate at Army HQ.

Army

World over, countries are pondering over the issue of providing maximum security to their nationals. Considering the growth of unexpected terrorism, natural calamities and intolerance among the nations, it is mandatory to involve each individual of the society towards national security and be of assistance to the regular army during any external or internal threat. To strengthen the efforts of our army, there are many new areas that can be included in the security matrix involving common citizens of the country. Some important areas are discussed in succeeding paragraphs.

Maoists Threat. Army needs to analyse Maoists threat in its entirety and involve itself through TA route. TA Sectors on the lines of RR Sectors can be raised in Maoists affected areas. Each Sector can have three to four TA units based on a mix of locals and regulars. These units can be eight company based units where 40 percent strength could be from RA on rotational basis and the balance 60 percent on TA concept enrolled locally from within affected states. These units will be a blend of Infantry TA and H&H TA units and should be affiliated to different regiments of Infantry. To make the program more attractive and sustainable, an understanding can be stuck with the affected State governments to simultaneously employ selected TA recruits in State Police/Home Guards or other State services to ensure their sustenance during disembodied spells. This may initially seem to be a little burden on States but the finances should not be any impediment as regards security and wellbeing of the people.

Information Technology (IT). TA units consisting of IT qualified people from civil society can be considered to be raised in conjunction with existing infrastructure of Corps of Signals. These specialists units will be officers heavy and their organisational structure and tasking has to be requirement specific and thus different from normal TA unit. Volunteer experts in IT field can be enrolled in TA as part-timers and contribute on security subjects as on required basis. They become a pool of reserves and can be employed on various projects required by the army. These specialists can work on programs that are identified by the army to counter possible cyber-attacks aimed at defence forces networks and war plans. Super specialists can be engaged to prepare proactive programs to penetrate into war plans and networks of hostile countries. Cyber spying needs to be given special emphasis in present day security set up where non-state actors are used by enemy states. Alternatively, IT TA units can be raised as covert units where volunteer members can be exempted military dress during their annual embodiments. Proper checks/balances and accountability need to be deliberated upon before enrolling members into these units. Location of these units can be at Army HQ and HQ Commands where enemy cyber threats are imminent and need effective counter measures.

Centralised Intelligence System. Valuing the importance given to intelligence and spying in modern warfare as also its reliance during Ramayana, Mahabharata, Kautilya and Shivaji's times, covert TA units based on loyal and dedicated people identified from the society, can be an excellent force multiplier for Indian Army. These people should be discreetly cultivated and enrolled by army. Such people may not congregate as a unit like other army units but should function under an umbrella organization for over all control of their tasking, actions, reports and welfare. How these units will be different from normal Intelligence Corps units is the absorption of people as enrolled part-time soldiers with assured career and related benefits of service. They are, concurrently engaged in their civil professions in the civil society. The organizational structure, tasking, command and control, training, employment and administration of these units need to be deliberately planned. Such units can be affiliated to Intelligence Corps of the army. To make it more task oriented, doctors can be enrolled as part of this force. These doctors while on army list as part-timers can be Centre/State government employees and are posted to sensitive areas where normally they refuse to serve for want of security and other facilities. Employing doctors on this concept will solve government's problem of doctors not volunteering to serve in remote areas and in addition provide information on the target areas, to the army. This will also work as an incentive for young doctors to serve in remote areas. The concept can be made more attractive if enrolment and service of doctors in TA is linked to their out of turn absorption in Centre/State Medical Departments. Eventually, even if a doctor enrolls himself in TA for five to 10 years, social and military aims are achieved. After their part-time engagement, if doctors are interested and found suitable, there should be provision of their absorption in Army Medical Corps.

Administrative Requirements. TA units based on part-time soldiers are required to be raised to function in emergencies as reserves for shifting of medical casualties and military logistics loads during war. It is experienced that during war, the medical staff is in extreme shortage and many precious lives are lost due to lack of timely evacuation. Medical Administrative Units of TA affiliated to Army Medical Corps (AMC), trained to deal with first aid procedures and shifting of casualties in midst of war will be very useful. Locations of such units can be along with field ambulances in combat zone. These units can be called as Medical Casualty Evacuation TA Units.

Another area where there is extreme requirement of specialists during war is Rail/Road heads where bulk stores pertaining to war are unloaded, sifted, reloaded and dispatched to the combat zone. Ordnance/Army Service Corps affiliated TA units can be the answer to address this problem. In peace times, the manpower of these units is embodied for two months for 'on the job' training as mandated under TA concept, and during emergencies or war, units are partially/ fully embodied as per ground requirements. These units in addition to performing their logistics tasks can also be utilized to provide trained manpower as convoy commanders and escorts while operating in Counter Insurgency (CI) affected environment. This will ensure big relief to regular troops who can in turn, concentrate on their operational task and training.

Navy

National security encompasses the security of people from all types of hostile activities aimed at threatening their existence and challenging sovereignty of the State. The aggressor can penetrate through land, sea, air and cyber space boundaries to cause damage and destablise a target State.

Map 4

India is a unique country to have both; land and sea borders to its credit. In addition to a land border of over 15,000 km with its seven neighbours, it has over 7,500 km coast line to defend. Along its coast line, there are numerous important communication centers and beaches. A smart enemy will try and exploit this lucrative flank to bring in simultaneity in his operations during war. The Indian Navy and the Coast Guard must have appreciated all possible threats as per their tasks and catered for each contingency. However, the world history is full of instances where enemy forces successfully carried out landing operations by surprising and overcoming defending naval forces of target countries. We have two potential neighbours who have capacity to surprise at crucial points. It is therefore imperative on our part to war game various options that the enemy can exercise to break our naval defence.

Territorial Naval Force (TNF) Units. There needs to be a ground force along the coast line that supports and supplements Naval and Coast Guard efforts in defending and defeating enemy designs. Careful appreciation of possible landing beaches has to be done to thwart enemy's plans of surprise. TNF units based on H&H concept, consisting of natives from coastline regions can be raised at identified areas. As the aim of raising these units would be to support Navy and Coast Guard during Hot War scenario, their role during peacetime would be minimal; and therefore, units raised on part-time concept of TA are ideally suited. During peacetime, personnel of these units are embodied for customary two month training and thereafter disembodied to continue with their local vocations. As regards their training, it has to be dual in nature – mainly under Navy and partly under Army at nominated Infantry Regimental Centres for sharpening ground tactics. The role and task should broadly include:-

- To defend identified beaches within Area of Responsibility (AOR) and destroy invading enemy forces venturing beach landings.

- To identify Dropping Zones in the AOR and destroy air/heli dropped enemy forces meant to link up and secure Beach Heads.

To realize above mentioned role, TNF units need to be suitably equipped and fully trained on the given equipment. They should be equipped with coastal mines, artillery guns, missiles, long range machine guns and anti-aircraft capabilities to defeat enemy designs. Such units, in addition to their specified task, will also be quite useful during peace time in disaster management tasks, anti-smuggling ventures by anti-national elements and any other unlawful activity taking place in their areas of influence. Also, their presence in the coastal regions of States affected with Left Wing Terrorism will have a deterrent effect on the free movement and unhindered operations by Maoists. These units will also be instrumental in defeating Maoists future plans, if any, of using the sea to their advantage for ferrying commanders, escaping and shifting of logistics, on the lines of LTTE of Sri Lanka. It will not be a bad idea to affiliate State Sagar Prahri personnel of affected States with TNF units for their two months engagement; for which period they will be paid for by MoD.

Port and Dock TNF Units. These types of units were part of Indian Navy after the independence but were later disbanded. With the ever increasing sophistication and rapid expansion of naval assets; both on and off-shore, there is a requirement of doubly guarding these assets. Whereas enough safety mechanism under the aegis of Off-shore Defence Advisory Group exists for off-shore security, there is scope to enhance on-shore security of naval assets. At present, civilians are responsible for the smooth functioning of ports and their security. These civilians do not come under Armed Forces Act and are free to have labour unions. Since important ports have to be functional round the clock, it is high time; Port and Dock TNF units are revived. This can be achieved in two ways. Firstly, the existing civilian manpower engaged on ports is enrolled and made into TNF units. These personnel keep performing their existing tasks during normal times as civilians and are only embodied during war, emergencies and any other eventuality of employees going on strike etc. This practice is being followed in Oil Sector by ONGC, IOCL and HPCL. While re-raising these units in Navy, earlier shortcomings and problems faced can be addressed by introducing new clauses. Secondly, MoD funded Port and Dock TNF units based on volunteer youth can be raised as an accretion to the existing manpower engaged at ports. During peace time, these people will be embodied for their two months training in a year; and in addition, can be embodied as on required basis. During war, they will be fully embodied for the period their services are required.

TNF Ships for Humanitarian Missions. TNF units consisting of specialists on humanitarian aid for disaster zones/ tsunami affected regions can be raised based on part-time concept. These dual task ships can be manned by specialists in the areas of medical, engineers etc and should be equipped accordingly.

Air Force

The air component of Indian Armed Forces was very small at the time of independence. It is also for this reason that application of air power in offensive operations was limited during 1947-48 war with Pakistan, in Kashmir. At the time of becoming Republic in 1950, IAF had six fighter squadrons, one bomber squadron, one Dakota transport squadron, one Air OP flight, a communication squadron and expanding training organization. Plans for major expansion in IAF were framed during the period 1953-1957[3]. Attention was also paid towards having Air Force Reserves; and consequently, Reserve and Auxiliary Air Force Act was passed on 14 Aug 1952. Based on this Act, following three categories[4] of reserves were set up:-

- Regular Reserves - consisted of ex officers and airmen of Regular Air Force.

- Air Defence Reserves - consisted of countrymen associated with aviation industry and not directly connected with Air Force.

- Auxiliary Air Force - consisted of citizens fond of adventurous life and ready for flying and technical training.

Out of the three types of reserves as mentioned above, the Auxiliary Air Force became the most popular as it provided adventure and opportunity to get trained and fly. For Air Force, it was a good chance to increase its reserves. Auxiliary Air Force was also commonly called as Citizens' Air Force or 'Week-end Flyers'. The recruitment to Auxiliary Air Force was open to all citizens on part-time basis and they could be trained to become airmen to fighter pilots. As a whole, the experiment was a big success. To accommodate part-time flyers, seven Air Force Squadrons equipped with HAL designed HT-2 trainers and Harvard were raised[5] at following places:-

---

[3]   History of IAF.

[4]   Reserve & Auxiliary Air Force from 'Territorials' (Maj Surender Singh's Blog) posted on 23 Nov 11 at 7.37 PM.

[5]   History of IAF.

- 51 Squadron, New Delhi (Safdarjang), 1955.

- 52 Squadron, Bombay (Juhu), 1955.

- 53 Squadron, Madras (Meenabakam), 1956.

- 54 Squadron, Allahabad (Manauri),1957/58.

- 55 Squadron, Calcutta (Barrack Pore), 1957/58.

- 56 Squadron, Bhubneshwar, 1957/58.

- 57 Squadron, Chandigarh, 1957/58.

Actual expansion and modernization of IAF started in the year 1957 and thereon; it began to be counted as world standard air force. After Indo-China war of 1962, Auxiliary Air Force Squadrons were also converted into Regular Air force Squadrons. Today IAF has a total of over 40 Squadrons of all types put together. However, this also seems to be inadequate in the absence of an enrolled, trained and strong reserve. The only arrangement that is in place today for emergency situations is air crew augmentation by sidestepping physically fit members engaged in staff, into flying squadrons. The war philosophy is changing the world over and reliance is shifting towards air power. In this backdrop, we cannot afford to have continuous deficiencies in our Air Force at any level. It will not be wrong to state that the Air Force of the past was simpler to handle with limited equipment at its disposal. Today, with introduction of each piece of newer equipment, the profession of flying is becoming more and more complex and interoperability is becoming difficult. Also, it is not possible to train reserve crew members in short spans of time. Therefore, it is in National interest to have plans to create trained pool of reserve crewmen and technicians who can be called upon to fill the gaps during emergencies. Revival of part-time reserve on the lines of erstwhile Auxiliary Air Force can be a step forward in this direction. In modern context, it can be called as Territorial Air Force. With ever increasing number of flying clubs and commercial airlines in the country, there should not be any problem of attracting the talent. Conversely, qualified youngsters in aviation will join Territorial Air Force units first and then make way to commercial stream. For their services rendered during embodiment durations, members of Auxiliary Air Force will be paid for by the MoD. Broadly two types of units can be considered to be raised:-

- **Fighter Squadrons.** These squadrons can enroll medically fit and interested ex Air Force personnel and volunteer crewmen from commercial airlines. Expenditure on this class of members for conversion and refresher training will be minimal.

- **Logistics Squadrons.** They can have people from commercial stream and interested/ qualified citizens from across the country.

The training for Territorial Air Force personnel should be planned as per their convenience. It could be based on weekly, fortnightly or monthly training schedules as per the requirement of the Air Force. Although attracting talent of required fitness will be a herculean task yet, if Territorial Air Force is revived, it can be a great success and an added asset to the Nation.

CHAPTER XI

REVIEW AND REORGANISATION OF TERRITORIAL ARMY

"...It is a proud privilege to be a soldier – a good soldier ...(with) discipline, self-respect, pride in his unit and his country, a high sense of duty and obligation to comrades and to his superiors, and a self-confidence born of demonstrated ability."

- George S Patton Jr

TA has reached its present level based on initial goals set for it by the British. It kept evolving with changing times and requirements. Many new areas have been added on; and likewise many were abandoned during its long journey. The growth of TA has been taking place in isolation in the past and was not really related to the growth of complete army. Growth is a continuous process and effort should always be to improve things for future. Inherent checks and balances should be in place to carry out periodic audit of any institution to timely ascertain degree of success vis-à-vis the target set.

It will be incorrect to conclude that a particular model adopted by an organisation at a given point and time was wrong. Need based growth is sustainable and durable. The end product will only be perfect and foolproof if it has evolved along with changing times. There is a famous quote by Shri Vivekananda on evolvement and gradual growth. He says, "the best timber can be had from the slow growing trees." This phrase is universal and applies to men and material alike.

The present organisation of TA is time tested and has paid the nation well. However, periodic review to evaluate the outcome, identify weaker areas and add new goals based on past experiences;

will be essential to enhance the future growth. It has been a general impression in the society and particularly in armed forces that even after having a long and rich history to its credit; the Citizens' Army has not been able to connect with the society to that extent where it could become a talking point amongst its nationals. Some sections of intellectuals and professionals still take it as one of the Para-military forces of the country. Needless to say, till recently, it was being projected as such in General Staff pamphlets of some of our Training Institutions. This is a cursory indicator about alienation of this wonderful concept from its beneficiaries – the citizens.

Review of TA

TA Review Committee is formed by the Government of India, Ministry of Defence to carry out re-evaluation of TA for its past performance, problems encountered and recommendations for its improvement and future employment. Since independence, three Review Committees were formed who gave their recommendations to the Government for implementation[1]. The members of the review committee are generally a mix of both; civil and army stream. The last such committee was constituted in 1995 under the chairmanship of Brig (Retired) KP Singh Deo who besides being a TA officer was also a Member of Parliament at that point and time. Ever since last review took place, many developments have taken place on the security front and TA is continuously being sought for prolonged durations. It is high time a fresh Review Committee is constituted to fully analyse all aspects of security situation in the country and suggest most suitable way of employing TA in future security spectrum. The following areas should be given as terms of reference to the future committee while it evaluates and formulates its recommendations:-

- Change in Role and Task of TA.
- Review of TA Rules/Act[2]. It should broadly cover:-
    - Anomalies in recruitment and enrolment in TA.
    - Clear definition and interpretation of Rule 33; used for embodying TA personnel for national emergencies.

---

[1] Coffee Table Book, Additional Directorate General TA.

[2] TA Rules and Act.

- Relevance of submission of 'No Objection Certificate' (NOC) from employer every year.

- Dichotomy in allotment of married accommodation to TA personnel.

- Regulations on clothing.

- Applicability and Promotion Exams.

- Promotions and connected seniority issues in case of officers.

- Aspect of placing equipment related issues of Non-departmental TA units under Infantry Directorate for ensuring uniformity and avoiding duplicity of effort.

- TA units as part of UN Peace Keeping Missions[3].

- Consideration of statuary instructions to government departments and civil employers to release their volunteer employees for TA and instituting bindings on departments/employers for honouring their employees' contributions to national security by compensating them financially and/or in promotions.

- Consideration of raising Women TA units as futuristic experiment.

- Raising of Armoured, Artillery and Artillery Air Defence units based on old surplus equipment.

- Raising of Field Ambulances (TA) to enhance capability during war[4].

- Consideration for raising other social sector TA units based on TA concept as covered in the book.

Present Organisation of TA

To coordinate the functioning of TA as an organisation, there is TA Directorate at Army Headquarters and a TA Group co-located at each Command Headquarter. The TA Directorate is headed by Additional

---

[3] IISS Strategic Comments-Redesigned British Army: smaller with more reserves. Volume 19, Comment 1- Jan 2013.

[4] Ibid.

Director General who is the advisor to the Chief of Army Staff on TA matters. Similarly, TA Group Commanders located at Commands are TA advisors to respective Army Commanders. There are permanent locations of TA units under each Command and these units have a clear task assigned for war scenario. There is no restriction, however, on employment of these units in other Command theatres for peacetime emergencies including Counter Insurgency threats. Other than H&H TA units which are area specific, Infantry TA units can be employed anywhere in the country and overseas. This gives added flexibility to the Army as an Establishment. The routine embodiment/disembodiment and relief program for TA is issued out by Army Headquarters on the recommendations of TA Directorate. At lower level, TA Groups ensure smooth movement, deployment and administration of TA units within their areas.

Need for Change in Organisation of TA

This aspect can be analysed at three different levels - Unit, TA Group and TA Directorate.

- **TA Unit.** TA at present has two types of units under its Non-departmental wing. These are Infantry Battalions (TA) and Infantry Battalions (TA) H&H. H&H TA units are area specific and have come into being in recent years. These are organised on eight company model. On the contrary, Infantry Battalion (TA) is of three types and organised on four, six and eight company models. Each type has a different Establishment to calculate manpower, equipment and vehicles. This model besides giving uneven representation to different regions also triplicates the work related to revising their establishments and actions related to demand/ supply at TA Directorate level. This anomaly also gives rise to difficulties in maintaining balance while planning embodiment/disembodiment and peace-field profile of units. The difference is glaringly visible during inter-unit professional as well as sports competitions. Another very important issue that needs to be addressed in TA unit establishment is posting of officers. TA is generally deployed in company strength and placed under command Regular/TA battalion deployed in vicinity. There is only one officer authorised in a TA company and this puts great pressure when the Company Commander is on leave or course. Unlike regular army Company, TA Company is commanded by a JCO in the absence of an officer.

- **TA Group Headquarters.** TA Groups located at respective Commands are yet to be included in the War/Peace establishment of Headquarters Command. Though co-located, they are yet to completely enmesh with the functioning of Command Headquarter. This causes delayed reactions within the branches and priorities pertaining to TA matters are, at times, not paid attention to. For non-inclusion of TA Groups as part of Command Establishment, their authorisation of staff, equipment and vehicles suffers and is not at par with other branches. This breeds an element of alienation.

- **TA Directorate.** TA personnel when embodied are governed by TA Rules/ Acts and in addition, Army Rules/Acts, as applicable from time to time. Their enrolment, employment and duration of engagement are different from the Regular Army. Because of these peculiarities, there are difficulties in perceiving TA as part of Army. Due to these misconceptions, it becomes difficult at times, to process various proposals related to TA matters within various Directorates at Army Headquarters. The lack of understanding on TA within concerned Directorates leads to slower movement of various proposals. Even ASEC, the body responsible for accepting/ revising War and Peace Establishments of units/headquarters, addresses TA's problems with same yardstick as that for regular army. This leads to stunted efficiency and momentum of improvement becomes slow. With expansion of TA canvas and inclusion of Ecological TA Battalions and Infantry Battalions TA (H&H), there has been increase in work load at TA Directorate. The difficulties are compounded with age old authorisation of staff which has not increased compared to the work load.

Proposed Changes in Organisation of TA

The changes that are required to be instituted in TA to enhance its efficiency can also be analysed at Unit, Group and Directorate levels.

- **TA Unit.** The following points can be considered to optimise effects of Citizens' Army:-

    - All Infantry TA units should be standardised and organised on eight companies[5]. This will make both; Infantry and Infantry (H&H) TA units identical in organisation.

    - With the embodiment periods of TA on rise and its continuous employment in CI/CT environment, there is immediate need of authorising minimum two officers per company. As such, with the proposed role revision for TA, increase in officers' strength will be essential.

- **Group Headquarter.** The following is proposed:-

    - There is requirement of early revision of War/Peace Establishment of Headquarter Command to include TA Group as its integral part. This can be on the same lines as TA Directorate is Part of Army Headquarters General Staff Branch.

    - For better integration in functioning, TA Group Commander should be the PSO of GOC-in-C. This will keep the Group Commander fully abreast with operational scenario and in better position to advise the Army Commander on employment of TA.

    - There should be a provision of posting one/two TA cadre officer/s in branches (other than TA Group) of Command headquarters to enhance contribution and cooperation.

- **TA Directorate.** The following changes are suggested:-

    - TA cadre officers should have representation in Perspective Planning, Military Training & Operations and Logistics Directorates. In addition, one officer should also be part of ASEC on part-time basis for better projection of TA problems.

    - Due to additional raisings like Ecological TA Battalions, H&H TA units and corresponding increase in ceremonial

[5] TA Review Committee Report 1995.

and training related activities, there is a requirement of creating two additional sections at TA Directorate. Newly created sections can exclusively deal with Departmental TA units and ceremonial aspects of TA.

- As TA has different rules of engagement and different training requirements, there needs to be a separate TA School to impart TA related knowledge to its personnel. A separate establishment is therefore, required to be approved for this institution to come into being.

- An additional post of DDG should be created to deal with Departmental TA units and ceremonial obligations including handling of media.

The broad organization after catering for all a/m additions will be as follows:-

PROPOSED ORGANISATION OF TA

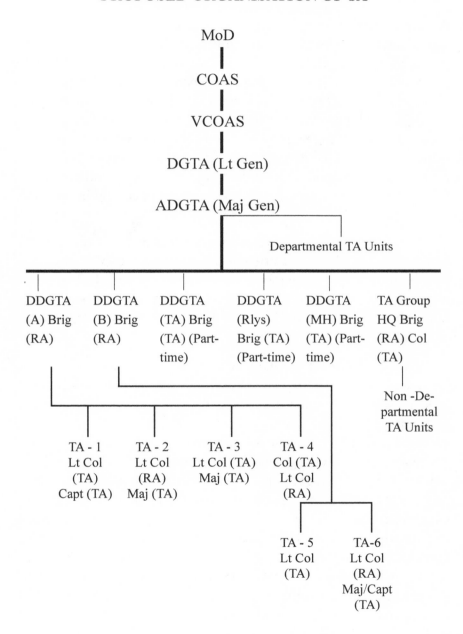

Anticipated Advantages of Review and Reorganisation on Efficiency

As mentioned above, a timely correction or a change in any organisation can provide ammunition to fight with functional problems plaguing the system. In case of TA, very minimal changes that have been spelt out in preceding paragraphs can bring about a radical change. The standardization of all Infantry Battalion TA on eight company model will bring in uniformity in functioning, training, expenditure, employment and equipment holding. This will bring relief at TA Directorate where things are planned. Similarly, the authorization of one extra officer in each company will take away the adhocism presently existing in companies operating in field and CI/CT environment.

The inclusion of TA Group into WE/PE of HQ Command is a rational requirement to bring in homogeneity, cooperation and coordination within concerned branches of Command HQ and avoid duplicity and delays. Posting of a TA cadre officer in any other suitable branch in the HQ will bring RA and TA closer for better understanding and results.

At TA Directorate, the work-load is very heavy to be shouldered justifiably by the existing staff. Creation of additional two sections as suggested will lighten the current load and bring in promptness and better execution under the new DDG. Also, to sharpen the knowledge of TA cadre officers and working skills of clerk staff on TA related rules and regulations; the establishment of TA School will be very helpful. Presently, TA has an ad-hoc School at Nasik functioning within the premises of one of the TA units. It has been an experience that proposals related to TA when moved through various line directorates at Army HQ are inordinately delayed for lack of knowledge on TA rules and regulations and sometimes returned with remarks not applicable for TA. The way out, to address this problem is, posting of TA cadre officers in concerned branches of Army HQ to bring in desired cohesiveness and mutual understanding. This will also give an opening to TA officers and those many regular officers will be spared to be posted back to their units involved in combat in CI/CT environment. Another very important place where a TA officer should be posted (can be part-time as per requirement) is ASEC. This will assist in proper assessment of requirements projected during reviews/extensions of TA establishments.

The review and reorganization to be done in TA need to be complementary to each other. There may be some critical issues which if included in the review will facilitate the functioning of the Study Team involved in reorganization of TA. Therefore, the canvas of the future Review Committee should be wide enough to include large number of problems that the TA is facing today. The reorganization should only be ordered on acceptance of TA Review Committee recommendations by the Government.

CHAPTER XII

RECOMMENDATIONS

"War will exist until that distant day when the conscientious objector enjoys the same reputation and prestige that the warrior does today."

- John F Kennedy

The concept of part-time participation by members of civil society in the Armed Forces of the country is as adventurous for them as is beneficial for the Nation. Shear participation by the citizens towards the security of the country; over and above their primary professions in civil street, sends out a sense of relief in the society and speaks volumes about their commitment for the Nation. It becomes the bounded duty of the Government to nurture this wonderful platform - TA; which connects the armed forces and the civil society and acts as a reservoir of force that is so badly required during any emergency. Talking of TA in a country where there is genuine requirement of a larger standing army to deal with its seven neighbours stretched over 15,000 km land border, should not be taken out of context. TA can always be expanded as an accretion to existing army strength to take over routine activities from regular forces so as to relieve them for their preparation for actual role. The strength of TA as a reserve will always be required whether standing army is expanded or reduced. It must be kept in mind that it is RA component which will be reduced if things improve and not reserve TA; as it is based on minimum liability.

TA can be taken to newer heights where it actually acts as an active force multiplier for the RA. For this to happen, people responsible for decision making have to seriously deliberate upon the basic structure of National security and ponder over the nuances involved. Debates and discussions at national level are required to be held, in addition to having various Study Groups giving their view points on strengthening the security fiber of the Country. The security of the country should be talked about like economy is discussed every now and then. An effort has been made in succeeding paragraphs to identify some rudimentary areas where the Citizens' Army (TA) can effectively contribute and play a role in nation building. The recommendations given; if critically seen can transform TA into a vibrant outfit capable of paying very rich dividends.

Society and Industry

A great intellectual and thinker, Dr Abdul Kalam, the ex-President of the Country had stated that large population of India needs to be seen as a great asset. It is true that the Nation is young and with the rising GDP and growth, the living standard of the countrymen is improving every day. With security of basic needs having been achieved, they very soon will go beyond looking at two square meals and start analysing issues that affect national security, economy, politics and image of the country in the eyes of outside world. They will want to involve themselves in nation building and other related issues of anthropology and culture. However, to shape the thought process of the society on these lines, visionaries of present generation have to sacrifice a little more to put in place required mechanisms that encourage people to think about our past history, glory, freedom struggle and requirement of being a militarily powerful nation. The start has to be made from schools where young minds are shaped; followed by villages and townships. The following is recommended to address important social issues:-

- There is a need to revise school syllabi across the Country to include chapters/stories related to our valour, honour and military ethics of the past centuries; and our present military standing vis-a-vis other countries of the world.

- Defence establishment has become more open to the society than before. Over the years, efforts have been made to bridge the gap and make it more accessible and people friendly. To further this cause, there is requirement of periodically organising military *melas* across the length and breadth of the country where military equipment and hardware should be displayed for people and children to see. These *melas* can be made more attractive by including children-games, documentaries/films on armed forces and other themes that trigger imagination in young minds. In addition, camps can be established by TA units in villages and remote areas to sensitise the population on TA concept and its advantages. This initiative will certainly help attract raw talent.

- The senior wing of the NCC should be linked to TA so as to motivate potential candidates at crucial times of their lives when they are deciding to choose their careers. Such candidates should be given coaching and prepared for their entry examinations for getting into the armed forces. This can be a step forward in overcoming the shortfall of officers in our armed forces.

- There is ample space to enlarge TA in arresting the regional based Maoist insurgency gripping some parts of the country. This is possible with the help of people's participation. Local people from the affected areas can be enrolled in TA units planned on H&H concept. These units will acquire required expertise in close quarter combat and jungle warfare. Battle blooded and after having finished their task of containing Maoism, these units will be a suitable force for sidestepping or for full time absorption into new formations that are planned for future[1].

- Considering the dire shortage of officers in the armed forces, a provision can be made through statuary order for enrolling specialists in the fields of Medical, Veterinary, Engineering, Horticulture and IT fields into TA units. They should be paid extra for their specialist services. These are the people who can be rotated and posted to difficult areas with GREF, TA and other units deployed on borders and difficult areas to give their services to deprived people as part of *Sadbhawna*. It must be appreciated that reserves in future are going to be crucial in areas that require less military training than frontline combat such as Trauma Surgeons or Cyber Specialists - that

---

[1] Restructuring the Indian Armed Forces by Maj Gen (Retd) GD Bakshi, Apr 2011.

are impractical to maintain in regular army[2].

- H&H Engineers based Disaster Relief units should be raised by each State. Personnel of these units during lean periods can be utilised for so many community related works within the State. By making provision of funds from schemes like *MNREGA* and *Pradhan Mantri Gram Sadak Yojna,* works like road construction, creation/revival of wells and ponds, construction of small bridges/culverts etc can be scientifically undertaken by Disaster Relief TA units in remote and difficult areas.

- Society is full of volunteer women who wish to join armed forces in any rank. An early decision should be taken to allow women entry in TA units as PBOR. This could be initially started with one company in each H&H TA unit. The concept is not new because in WW II, women from the Indian sub-continent were in forefront as part of Allied war effort. They made sure that men were relieved for combat duties[3]. The enrolment of women in TA on part-time basis will be a test pad for their suitability for army and a step towards their empowerment in the society.

- In India there are big corporate and industrial houses that have their business empires spread across the country in varied fields. It may be worthwhile to apprise them of TA concept. TA units/subunits raised under the funding of these big players could be a value addition. Skeleton staff from existing TA units can be posted for such units on deputation to meet their training and other administrative requirements. These units can be raised within the premises of interested companies and trained on Urban Concept (weekend training). The army will have the option of utilizing their services during operations by embodying them under MoD funding.

Government and its Departments. The following should be the line for Government and various departments under it:-

---

[2] IISS Strategic Comments – Redesigned British Army: smaller with more reserves.

[3] 'Women in Territorial Army', posted on a Blog by Maj Surender Singh on 13 Jul 2009.

- Fresh TA Review Committee should be immediately constituted by the Government to draw out a road map for TA's future expansion and employment. In fact, the best approach would be to constitute a larger committee that encompasses complete army for its restructuring and transformation. The TA review should also form a part of this Committee. This will help in better understanding and concurrent restructuring of both RA and TA and will lead to making comprehensive recommendations in the best interest of both. So far, independent TA Review Committee used to be ordered which prepared its report in isolation. As a result, some recommendations, at times, were not in consonance with the interests of RA; which later led to difficulties in convincing various directorates within Army HQ and in progressing cases. It is also suggested to set a periodicity of review committees fixed as 10 years and that of complete follow up on recommendations to take place within five years of approval of Committee report.

- Close analysis should be made of the recent proposals prepared by US and UK Army Planners on restructuring of their armies and reserve forces[4] and enhancing partnership between the two. Relevant models if found suitable can be emulated for own army. The empowered committee can also invite ideas from across the society on finding out the ways and means of improving societal participation in the armed forces of the Country.

- The Government needs to take initiative to involve big employers to find ways and means of facilitating participation of their volunteer employees in TA by sparing them on contributory basis for part-time engagement. Employers have to be convinced of timely return of their employees as mandated under TA rules and concept. To popularize this move, the Government may have to make a policy of compensating such employers by way of giving relaxation in income tax slabs, higher limits of investments in their

---

[4] Army 2020: Rationale for redesign, presentation by Maj Gen KD Abraham at IISS on 20 Nov 2012.

businesses and/or giving priority in awarding contracts and projects as per the number of people spared by them for part-time service. On the contrary, it is also recommended that if big corporate houses and employers do not wish to spare their manpower for TA, they should be liable to pay monetarily to the Government for national security.

- A statuary order needs to be passed by the Government as regards participation of Central/State/ PSU employees in the national defence. It is recommended that initial four to five years of Government employees; particularly those who will be later associated with Armed Forces, should be attributed to part-time service in TA. Out of this period, minimum two years should be their continuous embodiment in field areas along with their units. Adventure loving employees will grab this opportunity. On completion of their successful tenure with army, they should be compensated by one out of turn promotion in their parent department and/or additional increment in pay and pension. This effort will bring Government departments and the Army very close resulting into common work cultures, better understanding of each other's problems and fast disposal of cases pertaining to Armed Forces. For Class I officers of Government departments, the enrolment can be direct in the rank of Captain and the SSB route should be made optional.

- The Government should be sensitive about the importance of political leaders in the country and their massive impact on populace. It should encourage young leaders; both at Center and States to lead from the front and enroll themselves in TA. This will have a trigger effect on the population they represent. Political parties can go a step further by hailing the achievers by awarding suitable positions in their party sets up.

- Provisions can also be made by the Government to make it mandatory for PSUs and big employers to absorb percentage of disembodied TA personnel (PBOR) for their honorable sustenance.

- TA Cells/Nodes should be suitably super-imposed on existing State/Zila Sainik Boards for educating and sensitizing people on the concept of TA and informing them about recruitment schedules in various TA units of the area. Ex-servicemen can be informed by these cells about available vacancies in local Ecological units for enabling them to make use of such an opportunity.

• When restructuring of Indian Army is undertaken, it is recommended to bring reserves (pensioners till five years), DSC, NCC and TA under a bigger force which can be called as, 'National Reserve Force'. As of now, ex-servicemen reservists have never been recalled for any operations since 1947. It is recommended that these reserves should be annually called for minimum a fortnight for familiarization and training till five years of their reservist liability. This will enable the Army to keep an actual account of its reserves and plan their tasking accordingly. Coming to DSC, it is a separate entity under MoD. The role of this force is akin to TA i.e. to guard and look after the security of army depots, installations like DRDO, nuclear installations and VAs/VPs. Whereas the present strength of non-departmental TA is only under 35,000, DSC is 60,000 strong and by end of 12th plan is likely to touch one lakh. This force cannot be called as classical reserve force because it does not have a well-defined secondary role during operations. Both DSC and NCC make use of officers from RA for their functioning. It is very clear from its role and tasking that DSC is capable of undertaking guarding and protection tasks during war and peace. Therefore, it is recommended that tasking of guarding important military assets should be totally given to DSC and role of TA be revised to include defensive task so as to make a true force multiplier for RA during war.

• Considering the ground realities of unemployment and ever increasing requirements of security personnel in army, the enrolment and engagement mandate in TA needs to be redefined. The duration for mandatory embodiment in Active TA units should be made six months every year instead of present two months. The upper limit of service can be fixed at 24 years up to Havildar rank and only those who qualify to become JCOs should serve beyond this limit up to 28 years. This measure will enhance Army's capacity without any pension liability and also bring in little attraction for the cadres.

Armed Forces. The following proactive actions can be taken by the Army with regard to improving TA before forwarding any proposals for Government's ratification:-

• The role of TA needs to be revised on priority basis to include defensive operations for its active component – non departmental TA units. So far, TA is termed as second line of defence by virtue of its part-time nature. But with improved basic training and higher IQ of the modern citizen-soldier, the role revision will not be counterproductive for Army. As on today, in many holding formations, there are voids and BSF/CRPF battalions/companies is part of their defensive battle plans. It is any ones guess that when these battalions commanded by average trained CPOs can be relied upon by Commanders during war then why a TA battalion which is part of Army and being commanded by a senior infantry officer (generally a second command) cannot be relied upon for defensive battle. The only requirement is up gradation of equipment and little initial training.

• To harness the true potential of urban employees who cannot give their two months continuously every year for TA training, it is recommended to popularize and strengthen the Urban Concept of TA where they can come for weekend training. This arrangement can further be modified by permitting employees to attend two days training on weekdays in a month. This will persuade all those who always wish to devote weekends at home. As India is becoming more and more urbanized, the increase in Urban TA battalions is justified. As on today, there are only three battalions left (one in Delhi and two in Kolkata) where urban concept is partly being practiced. The point has been covered in Chapter I in detail.

• The trials on TA-isation for various models as suggested in Chapter VIII should commence simultaneously in active and peace formations. This exercise may take two to three years to fructify as TA battalions have to be suitably trained before being tested alongside regular units for field craft and defensive tactics.

- The internal and external reorganization of TA is urgently needed (Chapter V and XI). It is recommended to undertake reorganization of TA at all levels as suggested. This will lessen the present workload and enable the staff to focus on key issues affecting TA.

- Each border State is recommended to have H&H TA battalion/s for their local security and as deterrent against infiltration and smuggling bids.

- Scouts battalions of Indian Army generally have enrolment pattern similar to that of TA battalions (H&H). The only difference is their regular mandate and employment in offensive and defensive operations like regular units. On revision of role of TA, all Scouts battalions could be considered to be merged with TA to be employed as H&H units. This, in addition to saving some money to the exchequer, will also bring standardization of battalions engaged in similar tasks. In fact, Scouts battalions can be made as nucleus during conversion of TA battalions to defensive role.

- Newly raised Disaster Management battalions, presently operating under NDMA should also be brought under TA for better coordination of effort and footprint. Their training, employment and command/control aspects have already been covered in Chapter VI.

- Manpower identified in various arms and services as covered in Chapter IX, is recommended to be TA-ised. The trials for each should be given to different formations for validation.

- To bring in better regimentation amongst the TA cadre officers, their posting has to be confined to a cluster of three to four units. At present they are posted from one unit to another unit any number of times without any basis. This defeats the basic principle of effective command and control.

- The conversion of 3rd line transport battalions in the Army into part-time battalions of TA should commence under the supervision of competent Board detailed to oversee the changes taking place. More modifications on this can be suggested by the Committee proposed to be formed to deal with transformation of Army/TA.

- The establishment of workshops for repairs of vehicles and other army equipment by contracted companies should start on trial basis. These workshops have to be tactically located so as to provide maximum service to units with minimum travel and logistics effort. Outsourced workshops meant for repairs of transport, signal, IT, electric and electronic equipment should be capable of addressing all problems within the boundaries of Command. The work force working in these workshops should be enrolled in TA for war time eventualities. In normal times, they continue working with their employer and are embodied only when there are strikes or agitations in the organisation. During war, they are fully embodied. This will put a rider on the company concerned to always keep young and physically fit manpower at these workshops.

- The military transport being used at Category 'A' establishments, Static Formations of Army, Navy and Air Force should be returned and instead transport should be hired from civil as per the requirement in the organization. The civil contract can be given to a cooperative being run by ex-servicemen under the patronage of army. It should be made mandatory for this cooperative to employ disembodied TA personnel as drivers and technicians. Contracts have to be renewed biennially. This step will ensure large manpower saving and cost cuts. At present, if analysis is made, the maintenance cost in terms of manpower, vehicles, repairs and spares is colossal.

- It is seen from the experience that TA units are not sent abroad as part of UN Peace Keeping Missions. This leads to alienation in the TA cadre. TA units are affiliated to various Regiments of the infantry on the premise that they are adopted and treated alike other units of the Regiment. However, when it comes to incentives, TA is at the end of the line. Such step-motherly treatment indicates that the only interest left with the Regiments for their TA units is, few additional vacancies of Commanding Officers, officers and PBOR that are created by virtue of these units being there. Three TA units successfully took part in Operation Pawan in Sri Lanka[5]. TA of UK and National Guard of US contribute immensely in their UN missions. It is recommended that TA units be chosen for this noble duty on merit and trained to be part of UN contingents in future. This step will ensure a collective embodiment of a unit and its deployment as a unit under UN banner. Even if one TA unit is trained and sent on UN missions every two years, the training and confidence of TA fraternity will be sky high in next few years. Besides, the training and the experience gained will be very handy for dealing with homeland contingencies in future.

• Organisational loyalties are sometimes stretched too far in our armed forces. We, at times exhibit monopoly based approach. To take an example of the CSD facility, this has been given to armed forces and their families as an incentive in recognition of their difficult service conditions. This is being enjoyed by serving and retired personnel of armed forces. This facility, however, has been given to TA personnel with impractical riders. This speaks very poorly of policy makers who do not consider it necessary to grant this facility to Terriers who are on rolls and not yet discharged from their engagement. What additional difference will it make if sixty thousand beneficiaries of TA are added to already existing over forty lakh beneficiaries (serving and retired) of armed forces? This discrimination, on the other hand, is one of the causes of alienation in TA cadre and may dissuade citizens from joining TA. It is recommended that all TA personnel whether embodied or disembodied are treated like regular army soldiers for CSD facility. Similar is the treatment

---

[5] 'Citizens' Army', a Coffee Table Book on TA by Additional Directorate General Territorial Army.

given to TA as regards medical facility. A Terrier during his disembodiment period is not authorized any medical facility in armed forces hospitals. It is all the more reason that a person who becomes sick during his disembodiment period needs to be treated well at the cost of army if he has to effectively contribute on his embodiment.

- At present the mandate says that a person is eligible to join TA if he is gainfully employed. This was put as a rider when youth was not interested in part-time service and working people were prompted to join. Now, the situation is different and unemployed youth does not mind joining TA. The word, 'Gainfully Employed', should be scrapped from the eligibility criteria as it is no more relevant and is counter-productive. Instead, any unemployed who joins TA at his own steam should be given preference in Centre/State Government jobs to offset his disembodied period.

- As of now, TA cadre officers are not eligible to appear in Defence Services Staff College examination. It is recommended that the same should be made optional to them as well. Since lots of officers young in age are joining TA, they should be given level ground to compete; if they meet the criteria. Qualified TA officers if get approved to the rank of Colonel, should be given the command of TA battalions.

- Part-time specialists in the fields of languages, cultural issues and civilian reconstruction, as envisaged by UK and US as parts of their reserve forces, will be extensively used by them in their overseas engagements[6]. Specialist manpower of this nature for our functional requirements in overseas engagements should be enrolled as part of TA and can be embodied as on required basis.

- According to the Forest Survey of India report released on 07 Feb 2011, India had lost 367 square kilometers of forest cover in the previous two years. In 2011, India's forest cover stood at only 6,92,027 square kilometers which works out to 21.05 per

---

[6] IISS Strategic Comments – Redesigned British Army: smaller with more reserves.

cent of the total geographical area. Considering the success of Ecological (TA) units against rampant deforestation and illegal mining activities in Delhi and Uttrakhand, it is recommended that minimum one Ecological (TA) unit should be raised for each State to enhance the green cover. Participatory model involving local citizens of the area, as has been successfully tried in Assam, should be followed for long term sustenance of assets created. Also, as a step towards becoming 'Green Army', each Corps zone is recommended to have one MoD funded Ecological (TA) unit. These units will be based on ex-servicemen of the area for undertaking plantation and landscaping operations; tailor-made at times, to meet tactical and strategic operational plans.

- At present, Terriers of Ecological units are embodied for eight months in a year and are authorized very few weapons; primarily for their own protection. As discussed earlier, the funding of these units is made by either Centre or State governments. It is recommended that Ecological (TA) units be authorized adequate weapons and ammunition as per strength of each unit and provision be made to embody these units for two months every year for weapon/ field craft training within the realms of defence budget to prepare them to successfully execute their secondary role during war.

Media and Publicity

- The media needs to be fully dovetailed for propagation of TA concept in the society. As mentioned in previous chapter, a dedicated officer is required to be posted at TA Directorate to coordinate media and public relations. His charter of duty should include periodic visits to TA units and companies operating in field areas for their evaluation; and projection of good effects of these units on the society.

- It is recommended to organize discussions on television/ radio on local security related subjects where people's participation is essential. Experts on Service Selection Board and recruitment should interact live with people and answer their queries on entry into TA and other highlights of part-time service. TA icons like Kapil Dev, Abhinav Bindra, MS Dhoni and Sachin Pilot can be invited to give their experiences of being in TA and motivate people. Their appeals to people of the society will make difference in the younger generations for giving their part-time services for the security of the country.

- Almost all Army institutions except for TA, have their periodical journals taken out at different periodicities to highlight their achievements. It is suggested to start a TA journal on annual basis for better dissemination of TA concept into the armed forces and society. There are well qualified officers in TA who can happily take on this task for the betterment of the organisation.

- Specifically trained teams at TA Directorate/TA Group HQ level should be constituted to interact with final year students of professional and degree colleges to apprise them of the unique opportunity of being a part-time soldier/officer in TA. This approach will help TA enhance its reach deep into the society.

Conclusion

The concept of part-time service in the army by citizens of the society over and above their primary vocations is being given much weightage the world over. The systematic strengthening of this concept is in national interest. This ensures that members of society from various walks of life come forward to contribute in the effort of securing the nation. The Citizens' Army – TA, represents the complete society and its careful nurturing has much to offer towards national security. This is an instrument which involves the complete society in the defence set up of the country and creates an easily deployable reserve force during national emergencies. TA can manifest itself in numerous nation building activities besides being an active reserve component for the regular army as a war time measure. TA units can simultaneously be trained to be homeland security centric to be able to address unconventional misadventures by the enemy forces in future scenarios. It is appreciated that future wars will not be fought only on national frontiers; a smart enemy will concurrently engage all facets of our society to break the cohesion and will of the people. It is, therefore, essential to sensitise people of the country about such enemy designs and involve them in understanding the requirement of their being part of the overall security plan. It is high time the aspect of national security is discussed and deliberated upon by involving the complete society to help frame a fool-proof security mechanism. Volunteer participation by citizens in this mechanism will be crucial and bring in added strength to the regular army.

The economical, technological and social development of the country is only possible when the nation is militarily strong and the borders are secure from outside intervention. There is a greater need to push for measures that enhance efficiency in our armed forces and for that to happen, integration of the society in the defence set-up of the country is a national imperative.

BIBLIOGRAPHY

Bajpai, Kanti P, 'Roots of Terrorism', New Delhi : Penguin Books, 2002.

Bhisham, Pal , 'The Territorial Army', New Delhi : Tulsi Publishing House, 1983.

Chandra, Pranay (Editor), 'The Citizens' Army', New Delhi : Lancer Publishers and Distributors, 2005.

Codrington, G R, 'What is the Territorial Army?' London : Sifton Praed & Co Ltd, 1933.

Dogra, PC, 'Changing Perspective on National Security', New Delhi : Lancer's Books, 2004.

Dunlop, John K, 'The Territorial Army Today', London : Adam and Charles Black, 1939.

Edmonds, Martin, *Armed Services and Society,* Great Britain : Leicester University Press, 1988.

Gautam, PK, 'National Security A Primer', New Delhi : Knowledge World, 2004.

Green W E, 'The Territorial in the Next War', London : Geoffrey Bles, 1939.

Gupta, Shishir, 'Security Panel for Restructuring of Armed Forces', *Hindustan Times,* New Delhi : 19 Jan 2000.

Kanwal, Gurmeet, 'Indian Army vision 2020', New Delhi : Harper Collins Publishers, 2008.

Kanwal, Gurmeet. *'Army's Role in Nation Building'.* Defence & Security Alert, 2013 Vol 4, Jan Issue No. 4 60-63.

Kundu, Apurba, 'Militarism in India : The Army and Civil Society in Consensus', New Delhi, Viva Books Pvt Ltd, 1998.

Military Ethics : Reflections on Principles – the Profession of Arms,

Military Leadership, Ethical Practices, War and Morality, Educating the Citizen-Soldier, Washington DC : National Defence University, 1987.

Nayar, VK, 'Threat from Within', New Delhi : Lancer Publishers, 1992.

Oberoi, Vijay, 'Army 2020 : Shape, Size, Structure and General doctrine for Emerging Challenges', New Delhi : Knowledge World, 2005.

Ovejuna, Fuente, 'All Citizens are Soldiers', Delhi : Macmillan India Ltd, 1969.

Peedle, Bob, 'Encyclopedia of the Modern Territorial Army', England : Patrick Stephens, 1990.

Privatisation of Logistics Support Facilities, National Security Seminar, *National Security Series 1999,* New Delhi : United Service Institution of India, 2001.

Report of a Committee set up by H E Gen Sir Claude J E Auchinleck, Commander in Chief, *'Reorganisation of the Army and Air Force in India',* Vol I, October, 1945.

Roychowdhury, Shankar, 'Officially at Peace : Reflections on the Army and its Role in Troubled Times', New Delhi : Viking/Penguin India, 2002.

Saighal, Vinod, 'Restructuring South Asian Security', New Delhi : Manas Publications, 2000.

Singh, Prakash, 'Kohima to Kashmir : On the Terrorist Trail', New Delhi: Rupa & Co, 2001.

Singh, Surinder, 'The Territorial Army : History of India's Part Time Soldiers', New Delhi: Ocean Books, 2013.

The Army in India And Its Evolution, Calcutta : Superintendent Government Printing, India, 1924.

CPSIA information can be obtained
at www.ICGtesting.com
Printed in the USA
BVHW041019110523
664003BV00003B/72